VITIATION OF THE SCRIBES

VOLUME XIII

BY: TODD ANDREW ROHRER

iUniverse, Inc.
New York Bloomington

Vitiation of the Scribes

iUniverse books may be ordered through booksellers or by contacting:

iUniverse
1663 Liberty Drive
Bloomington, IN 47403
www.iuniverse.com
1-800-Authors (1-800-288-4677)

Because of the dynamic nature of the Internet, any Web addresses or links contained in this book may have changed since publication and may no longer be valid. The views expressed in this work are solely those of the author and do not necessarily reflect the views of the publisher, and the publisher hereby disclaims any responsibility for them.

ISBN: 978-1-4502-0946-5 (pbk)
ISBN: 978-1-4502-0947-2 (ebook)

Printed in the United States of America

iUniverse rev. date:1/26/10

When a loss is perceived to be an understanding then all eventual results encourage growth.

Mankind is afraid of flat ground not mountains.

I perceive:

11/29/2009 11:02:40 AM –
Native Americans, right brain influenced, were known for their ability to be expert guides and scouts. It is quite revealing that the sane, left brain influenced, would not use their own "kind" as scouts or guides unless the Native Americans were clearly above and beyond the ability of the sane in the area of scouting and guiding. It is perhaps interesting that the sane labeled the Native Americans as savages in many areas but when it came to scouting and guiding there was no one better than a Native American in that field. This is quite a red flag since the sane deduced the Native Americans were not very wise because they did not have the education the sane had, yet at the same time the sane could not find anyone who was a better scout in the universe. The sane actually used Native American scouts to assist them in tracking down other Native Americans the sane were trying to capture and of course at the same time the sane were suggesting the Native Americans were savages and unwise and not very knowledgeable. The sane had deduced that the Native Americans were not very wise because they were uneducated relative to the education methods of the sane and so it was acceptable to take advantage of the Native Americans and take their land and force them in concentration camps the sane decided to call reservations. The Africans, right brain influenced, were deemed property by civilization because they did not have traditional education and where placed in concentration camps called ghettos. Even beings in civilization, left brain influenced, who get education are deemed property and put in concentration camps called cities relative to:
"When we get piled upon one another in large cities, as in Europe, we shall become as corrupt as Europe. " - Thomas Jefferson
 The sane had deduced it is better to concentrate these beings into one location so they would be easier to control. The sane had concluded because they were able to take advantage of these beings it was proper to do so. The wisdom one can gain from the sane relative to their example is, if you are able to take advantage of someone it is proper to do so, no matter what. The logic of the sane is, if you see someone you are able to abuse or take advantage of, even if they are a child, you should do so because you are blessed by supernatural powers, and so anyone you are able to abuse, you have right too. The logic of the sane is any other human being who does not have their "brand" of education is obviously not human and so it is proper to abuse them and steal from them and harm them because the supreme judgment of the sane is that if a human being does not have the "brand" of education or enough of it the sane deem that human is clearly not human at all. If one does not have the "brand" of civilization, traditional education, then one cannot possibly be worth very much.

X = civilization's brand of education
Y = ones without civilizations brand of education
A = respect
B = disrespect

1

X = A
Y = B

This is quite an elementary equation but it is universally accepted in the land of the sane, civilization, the left brain influenced.

Civilization is in reality nothing more than a band of thugs that lives by their own backwards morals and delusional perceptions of compassion. Civilization will suggest it has compassion because all it did was steal all the Native Americans land, butcher many of their tribes into extinction, and then stick them in concentration camps. Because civilization did not butcher all of the Native Americans it will suggest it has compassion and cares for all human beings. Civilization will suggest they are not like that anymore, relative to treating ones without their "brand" of education properly, because they are not aware they will never be perhaps anything but like that. Civilization even treats its own kind in civilization poorly when they do not get enough of civilizations "brand" of education. Civilization is simply an abuser towards anyone who does not subscribe to its illogical rules that it calls righteous rules. Civilization will abuse everything in its path even its own offspring, and then come up with a law to convince itself its deeds are righteous deeds. One should be mindful at times a lunatic is unable to understand it is a lunatic. A lunatic will at times destroy something and then suggest it was evil and so it was righteous to destroy that thing or that being. A lunatic will oft create a code of conduct that will allow it to harm others and this way the lunatic will always perceive they are within the law or within a moralistic frame. The Native Americans were vilified by civilization and then civilization had the go ahead to destroy them. All civilization had to do was suggest "They are not like us" and that automatically meant the Native Americans were "evil" because anyone who is not like Civilization must certainly be evil, because it is impossible civilization could be evil, because Civilization is civil and one knows that because it's the first part of their name. Civilization is the god of civility so any group of humans that are not like them certainly must be the devil. The deeper reality is a person who gets the traditional education and has not applied the remedy to return to sound mind is under the influence of left brain so they behave a certain way and when they encounter a person who has applied the remedy or a person who never got the traditional education they see them as strange. In that respect left brain influence will always see a right brain influenced person as bad or evil because right brain traits are contrary to left brain in all respects. So a person from civilization who got education and has not applied the remedy is really just a left brain influenced and when they saw these Native Americans or Africans or various other "tribes" they saw them as bad because they were right brain influenced and so they saw them as less than they were so they took advantage of them. Because of that the person is not really as important as what influence mentally they are under. Left brain extreme people through history , ones who got traditional education and did not apply the fear not remedy, have always seen humans with right brain unveiled as bad or evil so the people involved are secondary to that reality. It is

2

not really civilization, left brain influenced, that took advantage of Africans and Native Americans, right brain influenced, as much as it was left brain influence saw right brain influence and disliked it because left brain see's right brain as bad because right brain is the opposite of left brain.- 11:48:07 AM

4:41:47 PM – Many long for truth but few know what to do once they find it. Seeking truth means one is seeking change. The truth will never conform to ones wishes for the truth demands one conforms to its wishes. What one does not seek is an indication of one's fears. If one gets what they ask for they must not be asking for much. Self is the worst enemy so defeating it will leave one with easy battles and not defeating self will leave one with losing battles. A rich man can give his money away and solve little but a poor man can give himself away and solve much. Great truth hides behind many layers of illusions so only a great fool can find it. Great truth hides from the rich and frequents the poor. Money cannot pay the bills that wisdom incurs. There are many rich people that will never understand wealth and many poor people that will never understand greed. Unleashing the mind is more important than enriching it. A tumor can grow but the seasons can change. It is better to change how ones see's than how one looks. Changing your perception changes the world and changing the world may change your mind. Altering your perception of the world alters your perception of the universe and that alters your perception of yourself. The truth is at the bottom of the sea and only a fool will keep swimming towards it after he has run out of breath. The truth is just beyond your reach so one should never define their reach. The truth does not want to reveal itself so one must find it accidentally. To become wise one must embrace foolishness. Somewhere beyond ultimate foolishness hides wisdom. Wisdom is not about always being right, wisdom is about understanding wrong. There is nothing wrong with being wrong as there is nothing right with being right. Most find wisdom on their last attempt. When one stops looking for wisdom they have found it. If one wishes to make peace with the world they must let go of the world. The world will not go anywhere if you let go of it. One cannot control the world they can only avoid being controlled by the world. An answer seldom reveals what one seeks like a question reveals what one seeks. The truth is everywhere it is just many cannot see it. The truth confuses the arrogant so seek humility. Surviving wisdom is more difficult than finding wisdom. One's mind can handle wisdom but ones friends can oft not. A great enemy will seldom lie to you and a great friend will seldom tell you the truth. If one asks their best friend what they think of them, one will often discover they need better friends. Great friendships are formed after great arguments are settled. It is not as important where you are at only where you perceive you are at.

11:33:05 AM –I have trouble finding fault with the ones who put me to sleep as the result of improperly teaching the sequential based education to me as a child and leaving me mentally unsound. I have trouble finding fault in what a person does when they are mentally unsound. I have trouble finding fault in the deeds of a lunatic. I at times want to seek vengeance but I cannot harm a lunatic because that would not solve anything. I cannot cast stones at a lunatic because a lunatic knows not what they do. I cannot cast stones at the ones who made that person a lunatic because they to, are lunatics and know not what they do. I have something called contrast. I understand how I use to be in the unsound state of mind caused by the education being taught improperly, left brain influenced, and I understand how I am now after negating that unsound state of mind by accidentally applying the ancient fear not remedy. If one only see's the darkness they will never understand daylight. I understand darkness because I understand daylight. Do your best to not get all weird because it's a very real prospect you have never seen daylight. You have to be mindful to give the daylight a chance because you may never have seen it, and so it may appear alien to you. I am not in a position to make demands because even if I convince you there is daylight you may not be able to reach it and experience it firsthand. That is an indication of the situation you are in mentally. Simply put you may be forever trapped in the state of mind you have been conditioned into by the left brain influence you call civilization because it pushed this traditional education on you as a child. I will do my best to explain to you every method I can think of that may get you out that trap but even then it is going to rest upon your shoulders to get out of the trap. I can explain to you the trap and explain to you how to get out of the trap but you must free yourself from the trap. I am not intelligent enough to determine who should be freed or should not be freed, so you are going to have to make that determination yourself. I will suggest right up front; if you do not detect you are in a trap you will perhaps never free yourself from that trap. If I cannot convince you of the trap I have failed you because you will never look for a way out of the trap if you do not detect the trap. Once you detect the trap or become mindful of the trap you will be able to start pondering ways to get out of the trap. I understand the trap because I escaped the trap but I assure you it was purely accidental. What that means is I was not aware consciously I was escaping the trap when I was escaping the trap. - 12:07:22 PM

12/1/2009 11:18:56 AM – I am mindful to include the music I create since the accident in the poor disguised diary attempts because right brain is known for creativity. When you hear the music you will come to understand my creativity is rather poor even at full power. This way even if you do not understand anything I write about you can still suggest you came away with one understanding from these poorly disguised thick pamphlet diaries.. I am mindful to attack this problem I am faced with from every angle because even though I will certainly convince you of the trap and of the remedy to the trap, but just because you understand the remedy to the trap does not mean you will be able to apply the remedy. The remedy or escape method to the trap is quite elementary in explanation yet equally difficult to actually apply.

2:09:25 PM – I am going to do some calculations in my poorly disguise diary and you do the best you can to confuse yourself by reading it.

The sane = Ones who are still in the trap, left brain influenced, unsound minds.

Lords or Masters = Ones who got out of the trap, right brain influenced, sound minded.

[John 13:14 If I then, your Lord and Master, have washed your feet; ye also ought to wash one another's feet.]
All the above means is the Master or Lords understand how to get out of the trap because that is why they are Masters or Lords, they got out of the trap and so once they explain to you how to get out of the trap they [have washed your feet], meaning they gave you back your mind because in the trap one has about 10% of a mind. So after a Lord or Master explains how you can get out of the mind trap, and you follow that direction and get out of the mind trap then you are a Lord or Master, right brain influenced, and you will assist others in getting out of the mind trap because you will know how to get out of the mind trap, and so you will be able to [also ought to wash one another's feet.] One cannot assist a Lord or Master in getting out of the trap because they already got out so once one gets out of the trap they assists others who have not escaped the trap to get out.
I am going to discuss this thing called the Lords prayer and so it is a prayer so to speak for the ones who escaped the trap and has nothing to do with the sane, who are still in the trap.

[Matthew 6:5 And when thou prayest, thou shalt not be as the hypocrites are: for they love to pray standing in the synagogues and in the corners of the streets, that they may be seen of men. Verily I say unto you, They have their reward.]

[And when thou prayest, thou shalt not be as the hypocrites(the sane) are] relative to [Revelation 2:9 I know thy works, and tribulation, and poverty, (but thou art rich) and I know the blasphemy of them which say they are Jews, and are not, but are the synagogue of Satan.]

Because you are in the trap you only see things as parts, a left brain trait is parts. There are many aspects of even these few words that require one to see holistically.
The first word is hypocrites. What a hypocrite is in relation to the ancient texts is a person who does something bad and perceives they are doing something good. Another way to look at a hypocrite is they know not what they do. So a hypocrite relative to the ancient texts is relative to these kind of people = The sane = Ones who are still in the trap, left brain influenced.
There are many words in the revelation comment you have to become familiar with because you only see things as parts.

Lords or Masters = Ones who got out of the trap = Jew = Christian = Muslim = Buddhist = Philosopher, right brain influenced, no sense of time.
The one reality one must first face is proof. The fact a person perceives time mindfully is factual proof their right brain ambiguity and paradox has been veiled so this mind has a strong sense of time as a result. A person who gets the traditional

education has a strong sense of time and that is factual proof their right brain is veiled and factual proof they are mentally unsound. If one does not understand proof when they "see" it they are doomed to remain in the neurosis caused by getting years of sequential, left brain based traditional education.

So all these people Jew = Christian = Muslim = Buddhist = Philosopher, are ones who got out of the trap. So then the comment [I know the blasphemy of them which say they are Jews, and are not, but are the synagogue of Satan.]

[which say they are Jews] . What this comment is saying is people can go on into infinity suggesting they got out of the trap, but that does not mean anything because it takes a bit more effort than words to get out of the trap. I wouldn't have infinite job security if all I had to do was tell you a few choice words to get you out of the trap. It would not be much of a trap if all one had to do was say some choice words to escape the trap. You are going to try your best to get it out of your head all you have to do is say a few choice words to get out of the trap and that way you will be slightly less delusional than you are now. This "assuming saying the rights word's is going to get you out of the trap" is what this comment means.

[Matthew 6:7 But when ye pray, use not vain repetitions, as the heathen do: for they think that they shall be heard for their much speaking.]

You can say "Save me from the trap" infinite times and it will not do anything in relation to saving you from the trap. You have to understand your ability to arrange word's is simply vanity, in relation to getting you out of the trap. I am writing these books to convince you that you are in a trap and even understanding that will not get you out of the trap.

[which say they are Jews, and are not] This is relative to a person suggesting they are something and then believing just because they say they are something that means they are that something. A person can say they fought in a war but the ones who fought in war can tell the ones who have from the ones who just say they have. One can go on into infinity suggesting they are one of these [Jew = Christian = Muslim = Buddhist = Philosopher] but that only means they can say those words and that has no relation to them being one of those labels. These labels denote an elite club that makes the most elite club you can imagine look like a boy scout troop. There are very few people alive today and very few people in the history of mankind who were true [Jew = Christian = Muslim = Buddhist = Philosopher] yet there are billions who will suggest they are one of these labels and have suggested they are one of these labels but all they really are is good at is saying those names. There are no classes in school to become a Lord or Master. If one gets lucky sometimes a Lord or a Master will take a few beings who are still in the mind trap and try his luck attempting to suggest to them how they can free their self from the mind trap. Some Lords or Masters, ones with no sense of time, right brain influenced, do not bother to attempt to assist ones to breaking free of the mind trap. There is no higher state one can be in than a Lord or Master, one of sound mind, so there is no reward for them assisting ones to break free of the mind trap. There is no higher rank in life than being a Lord or a Master, sound minded, so there is no reason for them to even associate with ones who have not yet escaped the mind trap. So because of that reality ones still in the mind trap can be certain they perhaps have never met a Lord or a Master and if they did they would perhaps never know it.

[Matthew 6:9 After this manner therefore pray ye: Our Father which art in heaven, Hallowed be thy name.]
[Our Father which art in heaven] =[Genesis 1:26 And God said, Let us make man in our image] so:
Father in Heaven = image in man = right brain, so right brain is the image in man that's name is hallowed. The reason its name is hallowed is because what you call civilization, hates it. I will rephrase that. Civilization, left brain influence, hates the image called right brain which is the image of the "father", in man. A better way to look at it is, every person has two hemispheres in their brain and the most powerful one by far is the right brain, so it is the father of the two hemispheres, and civilization hates it, and goes out of its way to make sure it is veiled or silenced.

[Matthew 6:10 Thy kingdom come. Thy will be done in earth, as it is in heaven.]
This comment simply means: let the ones in the mind trap get out of the mind trap like the Lords and Masters have escaped the mind trap. Earth = one in the mind trap , heaven = ones who escaped the mind trap,[thy kingdom come] means one gets out of the mind trap and they unveil right brain then they achieved heaven, sound mind, or become a Lord or Master. So this line could just as easily be, Let the kingdom come to the ones in the mind trap so they will unveil right brain and reach heaven, sound mind.

[Matthew 6:11 Give us this day our daily bread.] This comment is just asking for something to ponder or think about. A Master is a Lord of the mind or has sound mind so they are cerebral focused so they like to just think and ponder things. A better way to look at this comment is, give me a mental challenge today.

[Matthew 6:12 And forgive us our debts, as we forgive our debtors.]
 Some Masters have an obligation to assist ones out of the mind trap and it is very difficult to do that so they have a debt and the ones they occasionally assist with escaping the mind trap owe them a huge debt because once they assist one to escape the mind trap that person gets their sound mind back.
So this is simply the Masters saying, I am sorry I cannot assist more to escape the mind trap they are in and to the ones they assisted in escaping the mind trap, no charge it gave me a mental challenge, daily bread.

[Matthew 6:13 And lead us not into temptation, but deliver us from evil: For thine is the kingdom, and the power, and the glory, for ever. Amen.]
This comment [And lead us not into temptation, but deliver us from evil:] is a hex on the ones who are in the trap, ones who sense time, if they say this Lord's prayer. This hex is relative to this comment [Mark 8:34 And when he had called

7

the people unto him with his disciples also, he said unto them, Whosoever will come after me, let him deny himself, and take up his cross, and follow me.][let him deny himself,]

X = a Lord or Master who got out of the mind trap, right brain influenced.
Y = a person who has not gotten out of the mind trap., left brain influenced.
So this comment is translated like this.

[And lead us(X) not into temptation(Y), but deliver us(X) from evil(Y):] when spoken by a Lord or Master. So in that version it is simply saying keep the ones in the mind trap away from me and do not let them harm me.
When spoken by one still in the mind trap it's a hex.
[And lead us(Y) not into temptation(Y), but deliver us(Y) from evil(Y):]
It is a prayer relative to the ones who are in the mind trap to deny their self.
So one in the trap is saying, Lead me not to me and deliver me from me. So simply put one who is in the mind trap still is simply praying against their self(left brain influenced self). One is denying their self or hexing their self, self being the state of mind one is in, left brain influence, which is the trap.

12/2/2009 3:53:04 AM –When I was six I started education and this education reading, writing and math was all sequential based. Sequential is left brain trait. For example the ABC's are in sequential order and spelling words is simply arranging letters in sequential order and if you misspell a word you get a bad grade so one is conditioned to get very good at sequential aspects and over a short period time, a few years, their mind starts to bend to the left because left brain is sequential based. Mentally speaking what this left mind bend does is turn the emotions up and also turns many other aspects up because the cerebral cortex, hypothalamus and amygdala start sending out strong signals, and also false signals to the mind or to the being after all of this left brain conditioning/ education. There are ways to avoid this happening to a child and that is essentially oral education until the child gets older and their mind develops fully, perhaps, as opposed to strictly using written education. So I ended up with all these strong emotions and after ten years of depression and suicide attempts I had an accident. In my suicide attempt a year or so ago, I took a handful of pills and when I became ill my mind, hypothalamus, it controls fight or flight, said to me, "You are going to die you better call for help." I was so depressed and tired of living in that left brain extreme state of mind, unknowingly, and I simply said "I do not care I want to die." I then went to sleep and did not die, and about a month later I got this "ah ha" sensation mentally and now just over a year later, relative to a calendar, I am fully aware the reason I went through all the suffering was because as a child I was conditioned into this unsound left brain state of mind as a result of the education being taught improperly. I applied this ancient fear not remedy to the tree of knowledge, I did not try to save my life and I preserved it, or broke the left brain mind trap I was conditioned into as a child, accidentally, and unveiled my right brain after the education had veiled it and returned to sound mind. I can forgive that conditioning was done to me as a child because I am pleased I escaped the mind trap even though it almost cost me my life, however I am mindful what was done to me is still being done to children. I want you to understand you are in neurosis because you got the same education method I got and because of that you knowingly or unknowing mentally condition children into this bent left brain state of mind and leave a child in mental hell as a result, with a veiled right brain. You have been conditioned into an unsound state of mind just like I was and you are perhaps unable to escape the mind trap, and I understand that because I escaped accidentally, so all you are doing in your life is continuing to mentally harm innocent children's minds knowingly or unknowingly, just like you did to me. You are in neurosis because of the conditioning you got as a child, and so you are mentally harming children and putting them in a mental state of hell, and you are in too deep of neurosis, mental hell, to perhaps even believe you are doing that to children. - 4:21:53 AM

1:16:59 PM – I wake up and I have moments of frustration because I realize I am never going to make any progress in convincing lunatics they are lunatics, and the lunatics are just going to keep mentally hindering innocent children with the sequential based education because the lunatics have no idea what they do to innocent children's minds and so I am mindful that I am not concerned what I write in my books because I perhaps cannot reach lunatics, for they are perhaps mentally too far gone. I understand I use to be a lunatic and I accidentally broke free of that mind trap civilization put me in as a child. I am compelled to convince my friends of what they do to children with their sequential based education when taught improperly. I am in a cycle where I run full speed into this granite wall and I am unable to ever make any progress and after a short amount of time relative to a clock I make another run for the granite wall. Right brain loves impossibility but as for me I am in neutral mentally and so I do not suffer and I am at the stage I hardly feel a thing one way or the other. If I had emotions I certainly would be forming an army to try and stop you from doing what you do to innocent children mentally but I am indifferent at this point. I would destroy myself if I cared so I will not care. I will watch civilization, left brain influence, mentally ruin children, right brain influence, with their sequential based education being taught improperly into infinity and I will keep a smile on my face. I will just assume I am being tested to see if I can keep my head when all the lunatics around me are harming children. I will keep my cool in the face of horrific mental abuse of innocent children. One should be mindful I speak in paradox, a right brain trait. - 1:46:22 PM

5:01:13 PM – I defeated my fear of death and in doing that accidentally, the hypothalamus, cerebral cortex and the amygdala were shocked back into working order and this unveiled right brain after it was veiled by the many years of left brain sequential education. The machine, right brain is now in an infinite loop of contradiction.

X = the boat which is the species

Y = amount of children being conditioned into the unsound left brain state of mind as a result of the education being taught improperly on a yearly basis.

Z = amount of people I can convince to apply the remedy, the method to negate the unsound left brain state using the fear not remedy

The reason I am in this contradiction state is because I cannot convince as many people to apply the remedy(Z) as civilization, left brain influence, will create who need the remedy applied(Y) on a yearly basis. I am bailing out the boat (X) with a tea spoon (Z) and civilization is pouring gallons of water(Y) back into the boat(X) at the same time. What this means is my right brain is fully aware it cannot win and is fully aware it can only lose but it has already started the infinite loop in relation to attempting to bail out the boat with a spoon while it is aware gallons of water are being poured into the boat at the same time. There is a concept called know when to quit or know when to fold them. Right brain is a machine and it not concerned with morals.

Right brain is not interested in morals because morals suggest quitting and right brain does not quit because right brain is a machine. Right brain is not concerned with looking good and is not fazed by looking bad. The machine does, and is not looking to do something until its finds an end it is only focused on doing something. A better way to look at right brains mindset is, there is no beginning and there is no end. There is no end because there is no beginning. Right brain has determined impossibility in bailing said boat out and so it is pleased because it found something it can never win against and so it can simply use that impossibility as a means to keep getting better. Left brain is always looking for an end in sight and contrary to that right brain does not acknowledge a beginning or an end. I will try to convince myself that my cause is hopeless and I can never convince society the bad mental side effects that all the sequential left brain written education has on the delicate mind of an innocent child and my right brain will suggest I should write that down in the book because it makes good filler. So I am unable to stop the right brain because it is a machine and it has already initiated the infinite loop program. Right brain is not allowing me to sense fatigue or emotions or depression relative to this situation. Right brain is not allowing me to have a say because it continues to convince me to keep writing no matter what regardless of what happens to me as a result of writing what I write. I am mindful what I write about is a huge can or worms but right brain will not let me be concerned about what this may all lead to relative to my well being. Because right brain has put me in the "now" I cannot think of any plans to trick it to stop because I can only operate in the now. I oft get the impression right brain has found an impossible problem and nothing else matters because it's a machine and it loves impossibility. I am mindful at times I try to act mean and I try to act funny but I am always reduced back to the machine state which is the now or neutral. The reality that the education being taught improperly ruins the mind is absolute fact but even saying that will not allow me to get out of my isolation chamber to go do something about it. I should be up in arms about what I am aware this education does to children but I am not up in arms because I have infinite books to write and that is paramount to everything else including me, but of course I speak in paradox, a right brain trait. My right brain will not allow me to maintain happiness or sadness or satisfaction or dissatisfaction and that is relative to its no beginning and no end mentality. I should be ashamed to publish books of such poor grammar quality but I understand right brain is not even concerned if anyone else in the universe can understand what these texts say because right brain understands what these texts say. Right brain will not let me feel emotions more than a second or two because emotions would simply get in the way of its infinite loop purpose. I am not concerned about anyone else because I am unable to stop the machine and the machine has the last word on everything relative to me. I am aware I should be taking a break and not writing so many books so fast. I am aware it certainly must be taking a toll on me but I do not sense any fatigue or any stress at all so I just decide to keep writing. Right brain is telling me to keep writing until I drop and I am unable to sense when I may drop. I cannot tell if I am overdoing it at all. I have no sense of fatigue and then right brain will suggest I should write that in the book because it will make good filler. So before I can go on a crusaded to save the world from itself I have to figure out how to convince the machine to turn off the infinite loop it has initiated and I understand I am powerless to do that. Right brain has decided to tell the world everything about everything and it is not even important if the world understands what right brain suggests because that would suggest an end. The less people understand what right brain is saying in these texts the faster it will write these texts. I am mindful I am attempting to convince the world about something I do not want to convince the world about. I am mindful I want you to understand and at the exact same time I do not ever want you to understand. I am mindful right brain no longer even acknowledges the world or civilization as anythingmore than a medium to speak to but is not concerned if it actually gets its message across at all. Some may ask what is the point then, and the point is infinity. - 5:37:34 PM

12/3/2009 6:40:20 AM – Perhaps God is right brain relative to [god made man in his image] and the [kingdom is within.] So perhaps God is complexity, intuition, paradox, random access and ambiguity which are all traits of right brain. So the adversary of God is left brain, sequential based, simple mindedness and slothful; in contrast to God. So this is what kills God in man:

"If you reflect back upon our own educational training, we have been traditionally taught to master the 3 R's: reading, writing and arithmetic -- the domain and strength of the left brain."
The Pitek Group, LLC.
Michael P. Pitek, III
President

So traditional education, the tree of knowledge, is simply a method to kill the god aspect of a human when taught improperly. Kill is an absolute but a better way to look at it is to veil or hinder or hide or deny the god aspect in man. God is perhaps the right brain so perhaps there is no god floating in the clouds because god is the cerebral or spiritual reality not the physical reality, thus the comment god is in all men, humans, but traditional education "kills" god in most beings. The physical reality is left brain domain or physical based. This again is a contrary. Right brain is cerebral and left brain is materialistic based. One may assume I am biased against left brain but that is not truth. Left brain is so weak one has to actually get this : "If you reflect back upon our own educational training, we have been traditionally taught to master the 3 R's: reading, writing and arithmetic -- the domain and strength of the left brain." and when they get this thing called traditional education it favors left brain and after even a few years of this left brain conditioning, right brain becomes veiled, so left brain is at about 90% and right brain is at about 10% so one in fact is of unsound mind, and even at that disadvantage right brain still comes out at moments and people still have moments of clarity and moments of creativity, a right brain trait, but it tends to be the result of drugs use or traumatic experiences. So one has to look at the left brain conditioning like scales.

X = left brain
Y = right brain

After the education starts at the age of six the scales start to tip in X's favor and the more education one gets the more the scales tilt in X's favor and thus the more veiled Y becomes. By the time a child is at ten or twelve their right brain is veiled, so their mind is like a crescent moon. The left represents the black slothful sequential based aspect of said moon and the light sliver is the complex right brain. So relative to the ancient texts sinning against god is this : "If you reflect back upon our own educational training, we have been traditionally taught to master the 3 R's: reading, writing and arithmetic -- the domain and strength of the left brain."
 God is perhaps right brain and that "brand" of education veils right brain so it attacks and turns off right brain so it is a sin against God. This is not suggesting education is bad it is suggesting education is tool and if not taught by a master who understands the potentially devastating mental side effects, the tool education is the worst mentally damaging invention in the universe. One who does not get any traditional education at all will be mentally better off than someone who does get traditional education. If a child does not get any of the reading, writing and math then their right brain will not be veiled and so when they start to get that education after their mind matures perhaps around the age of eighteen they will pass up the person who gets all that traditional education within a year and that is an indication of how powerful right brain is. I understand I have figured out the core problem of mankind relative to this education relative to the last 5000 years and I did it all alone and for only one reason. Right brain has pattern detection, intuition, complexity and its pondering or calculation ability is as fast as the speed of thought and that's is how I accomplished this feat. It is not me. It is right brain is a powerhouse beyond description. I do not need to go get educated because I

can educate myself in a fraction of the time because I accidentally unveiled the machine. I am not wise, I simply accidentally unveiled my right brain, after it was veiled because of the education, and it is so powerful I can only suggest right brain is unnamable in power. I am suggesting you have a right brain and it was veiled because of the traditional education and all you have to do is apply this ancient fear not remedy and you will unveil it and then you will understand it is not me, it is right brain. You perhaps have to get it out of your head that the things I suggest or mention are because I am wise. You perhaps have to get it into your head all I did is unveil right brain after traditional education veiled it.

Your are trying to conclude right brain is just as powerful as left brain but the reality is right brain at 50% and left brain at 50% which is sound mind means right brain is the dominate of the two hemispheres in relation to effecting ones concentration abilities and ones perception. When both hemispheres are at 50% right brain is the dominate one because it deals in random access thoughts, pattern detection, intuition and complexity and contrary to that left brain deals with intellect, sequential thoughts and is thus simple minded in its nature in contrast. The mind needs some of the aspect s of left brain but in general it relies on right brain when both hemispheres are equal in power. Left brain plays second fiddle to right brain when both are at 50%. When one is conditioned by education they tend to see things as parts and that is a left brain trait, and that is an indication right brain is so veiled one's mind is living under the power of the left brain traits but when right brain is unveiled and at 50%, then one sees things holistically so the 50% left brain, seeing things as parts aspect is not dominate. One would think at 50/50 both hemispheres would be equal in power or influence but that is not true because right brain is the dominate of the two when both hemispheres are at 50/50.

All the people you know that are known as teachers of said traditional education are clueless and all the people you know as the board of education are totally clueless about the bad mental side effects of the education because they got the education also. They are of unsound mind and they simply harm children because they perceive this education which favors left brain could not possibly harm the mind of an innocent child after many years. They are clueless. They are what are known as the blind creating more blind. The deeper reality is all of said people got the education so they are influenced by left brain and left brain only wants to make everyone else left brain influenced and they see a child, who is right brain influenced, sound minded, as bad and these left brain influenced people want to "fix" that child and make that child like they are, left brain influenced.

"we have been traditionally taught to master the 3 R's: reading, writing and arithmetic -- the domain and strength of the left brain." All this is saying is education, the traditional form of education is simply a mind altering invention, and the only thing one can possibly gain from this traditional education is an unsound mind at the end of the day.

If you want to get religious this "we have been traditionally taught to master the 3 R's: reading, writing and arithmetic -- the domain and strength of the left brain." is how god is killed in man.

Since you got the education your mind is bent all the way to the left so you are only capable of simpleminded sequential thoughts and your ability to understand complexity is essentially veiled, right brain is the complexity aspect of the mind. You should think what I am saying is wrong or not possible because your thoughts cannot perhaps tie up all the loose ends in what I have just explained and your right brain intuition is all but gone.

You are perhaps attempting to defend education because your intuition, a right brain trait, is silenced and so you are trying to use your left brain intellectual aspect, and what that means is you have never read anywhere that's states absolutely, traditional education harms the mind to a devastating degree, until now, so you are coming to sequential conclusions that what I suggest cannot be truth. Because your right brain intuition is veiled you are forced to use left brain intellect and what that means is you cannot think for yourself using intuition so you have to be told or you have read what to think. Simply put you have to read what other people say to form an opinion because your intuition aspect is veiled so you have to be told what to think about everything by others. You have been told, education is flawlessly good and so you have never questioned it, and since you have no intuition powers you will perhaps just assume what I am suggesting is wrong.

The reason you're in a mind trap is because the only people who can escape this left brain mind trap are outcasts relative to reverse world, civilization, left brain influenced beings, the world of the ones with left bent minds. I have no credentials. I am not credible relative to reverse world. I didn't get taught what I explain to you. I unveiled right brain and it taught me everything I tell you. Right brain detects patterns and has intuition so in one year relative to a calendar I have figured out everything there is of value to figure out relieve to the history of mankind by myself just by detecting patterns and using intuition to formulate those patterns into a meaningful understanding. That is perhaps hard for you to grasp because your right brain is veiled and so you would conclude if what I suggest is true then education itself is essentially vanity or meaningless or simply brainwashing and thus mentally hindering. You are unable to understand how powerful right brain is when unveiled because your right brain was veiled by the time you were ten and so your mind was not even warmed up, developed, before your right brain was veiled, so you have no experience with right brain being unveiled and at full power, fully developed. There is no way in the universe you could know what your mind is like when your right brain is unveiled and because of that you are trapped. I did not unveiled right brain because I am so wise I unveiled right brain because I am a fool. I did something foolish relative to the reverse world and it turned out to be something infinitely wise relative to reality. Because of that I can never say I am good. I cannot claim the accident is my conscious intentional doing. - 7:17:44 AM

12:49:17 PM – There is a concept in the reverse world called prophet, saint, messiah, the one, the messenger and this is all one actual thing. The reverse world idolizes these beings because they perceive consciousness is special. A better way to look at it is the ones in reverse world got the traditional education and so their right brain is veiled so when they see a person who has unveiled right brain they assume that person is special. So reverse world idolizes beings that break out of the mind trap traditional education puts them in. So the definition of a messiah, a saint, a prophet, a messenger is simply a human being who breaks out of the mind trap traditional education put them in and once they do that right brain assists them in figuring out what the traditional education did to them mentally and then they dedicate their life to trying to explain the mental effects of the traditional education on the mind, and the remedy, the key to negating those unwanted mental side effects. Anyone who does not understand that has not applied the fear not remedy fully so they still have right brain veiled and so the intuition and pattern detection of right brain are not powerful enough so they can't understand the definitions of those words which means they are still under the influence of left brain. Can't, denotes their mind is unable to grasp that complexity because their mind is not at full power. This is an indication of how difficult this left brain bent state of mind, the mind trap, is for one to escape from but it is also a paradox.

It is very easy to escape from the mind trap.

It is very difficult to escape from the mind trap.

It is very easy because it is a mental exercise of self control and once one is in the ideal situation it takes one second to apply and it is totally painless.

It is very difficult to escape from the mind trap because getting to that ideal situation requires one to deny what their perception is telling them.

It is simple to escape from the mind trap and at the same time it is nearly impossible to escape from the mind trap and for some it is perhaps impossible to escape. One has to be mindful that the many years of left brain education has altered their perception so essentially ignoring ones perception in the right situation is the key to escaping that left brain bend mindset.

X = ones perception after the years of traditional education, seeing parts
Y = the sound minded perception which is a symptom one has escaped the X mind trap, seeing holistically.

X is the reverse of Y. This is what is known as the reverse thing or relative to the ancient texts the anti-truth or anti-Christ. This reverse thing is the boundary that keeps a person from escaping the mind trap caused by the years of traditional education. When a person is in the X state of mind they will see the door to Y state of mind as a wall. A person in X state of mind will not see the door to Y state of mind as anything but a wall. So the only way a person in X state of mind can escape is to run into that wall and what that means is they have to deny their perception that suggests that wall is a wall. Once a person in the X state of mind understands that wall is in fact a door they will have to understand they are seeing doors as walls so they are hallucinating. That requires humility and that is difficult for them to accomplish in the X state of mind. I am not suggesting you are hallucinating because that is your nature from birth I am suggesting you got years of traditional education and that has altered your perception and that is why you are hallucinating. I am suggesting a cause and effect relationship. I am suggesting you took a hallucinogenic unknowingly and now you are hallucinating. I was hallucinating just like you are hallucinating but I accidentally broke free of that mind trap of hallucinations, perception, and I am trying to explain to you how I did it so you can break free of that hallucination mind trap also. That may make it seem like I have morals and I am trying to be a good Samaritan but that is an illusion. I do not perceive I am assisting you because I already understand fully you perhaps cannot escape from the mind trap you are in and because of that it would harm me if I tried to assist you because I am already fully aware you perhaps are trapped for the duration, of course I speak in paradox. It would harm me to mindfully assist you because I am fully aware you have fallen into a place that I perhaps cannot reach to assist you. Some people climb mountains and they fall into an accessible place and they can be rescued, and some people fall into inaccessible places and they cannot be rescued. Some people get cancer and when it is discovered, it is too late for them. The doctor has to tell the patient they caught the cancer but not in time. There are ones with the cancer that was caught in time and ones with the cancer but it was not caught in time. A doctor would harm himself if he tried to save a patient he already knew had cancer that was too far in its progression, so that Doctor has to disassociate himself from that patient to avoid harming himself. I have to mindfully look at you as an illusion because I understand you have fallen into a place and I may not be able to reach you. Because of that I am not a good Samaritan I am selfish. I understand if I try to rescue you from the place you have fallen I may harm myself and I am not willing to do that so I must consider you as lost. This mindset is relative to me. There is a battle field and many injured people on that battle field. Some have fatal wounds and some do not. I cannot spend my time on someone with a fatal wound because then someone with a non fatal wound may suffer as a result of that. I have to determine swiftly if someone has a fatal wound or not, and in order to do that I have to not be emotional. I cannot assist everyone on that battle field because some have fatal wounds so I must consider them lost causes. I must think clearly to determine who has fatal wounds and that means I must not have emotions because emotions would cloud my concentration. I would be pleased if no one had fatal wounds on that battle field, but that is not reality. I must stay in reality and reality suggests the vast majority of people on that battle field have fatal wounds. I am mindful only a small fraction of the people on that battlefield can make it back to the hospital. I am not pleased with that but that is reality. One cannot create reality one can only attempt to understand the reality of the situation. I can detect the patterns of the battlefield and deduce what reality is from those patterns but I cannot create the patterns, I can only detect the patterns. One must be a good judge before they can be a good Samaritan on a battlefield full of fatally wounded people. - 1:38:19 PM

Old friend - http://www.youtube.com/watch?v=shCnh5lIT8Y
I can't patch you up
I can't life you up old friend.
Rest your head old friend

It's the end old friend.

3:56:23 PM – This is psychologically and neurologically what this remedy does to the mind.

X = left brain state after the years of left brain education
Y = post remedy when the right brain becomes unveiled and the mind returns to 50/50, harmony, left and right brain equal.

The years of traditional education bends the mind to the left or favors left brain. A side effect of that is in part the hypothalamus gets stuck in this state of sending very strong fight or flight signals. Because of that one becomes afraid of many things they should not be afraid of like words, nudity, music, bad hair cuts, the dark, what others think of them and what one thinks of their self, and their thoughts. These fear symptoms sometimes appear like shame, embarrassment, shyness but they are not really those things, those emotions are symptoms of fear caused by the hypothalamus sending very strong signals because the mind has been bent to the left because of all the years of sequential based, left brain, traditional education.
So the remedy is one gets into a situation to make that hypothalamus give the strongest reading it can give and that is death and then one ignores that strongest signal the hypothalamus can give and then that knocks the hypothalamus out of it false signal sending. Once that is done the mind is clear of all those strong false signals and then the right brain can unveil itself, then waking up begins.
So the traditional education bends the mind to the left and the hypothalamus starts sending very strong fear signals and both of these things keep the right brain veiled and so one has to fix the hypothalamus with the fear not conditioning and then the right brain is unveiled. The biggest problem with accomplishing this is the person has to understand their hypothalamus is sending them false fight or flight signals. The hypothalamus is telling a person in the X state of mind a shadow is going to kill them literally and that person has to understand that is not true so they have to just ignore it and that is the remedy and that is what is known as self control. One has to not allow their thoughts to control them for that one instant they are in a situation that hypothalamus says a shadow is going to kill them and that fixes the mind. The complexity here is one in the X state of mind is going to believe that shadow is going to kill them because they are trapped by their perception and hallucinating. One has to commit treason against the signal the hypothalamus is sending them, and that requires self control. It is a one time, one second thought process and it is painless and then the mind will return to normal or sound mind or the right brain will unveil shortly after. One in the X state of mind believes all their hypothalamus signals are absolute reality when in reality the signals are oft false. This is why the ones in X state of mind are trapped by their own perception so they are their own worst enemy. One in X state of mind is keeping their self trapped because they are assuming the signals sent by the hypothalamus are all true. It is one thing to be in a shark frenzy and hypothalamus sends a fight or flight signal and it is another thing to be in a dark spooky location

and the hypothalamus sends that exact same fight or flight signal. It is one thing to get a fight or flight signal in a shark frenzy and get the same signal when one says a perceived bad word or cuss word. The hypothalamus in a person in the X state of mind is giving false positives on just about everything. Persons in the X state of mind won't say a cuss word because they believe they will die, they won't eat certain food because they believe they will die if they do, they won't listen to certain music because they believe they will die if they do. There is no evidence in the collective knowledge of the species that listening to a certain song will kill you nor eating a certain piece of food will kill you, nor saying a cuss word will kill you, but anyone in the X state of mind still believes it can kill them so they are in fact hallucinating. Everything is relative to the observer so an observer that is hallucinating will act on those hallucinations and believe they acted properly. It all comes back to one thing only. If you do not believe and you do not have faith that many years of sequential left brain education, which is traditional education, bent your mind to the left, you are trapped forever by your own perception. It is not possible you could get the years of left brain sequential education you got, and come out with a sound mind, as in left and right hemispheres are both 50 % active. It is impossible to come out with a sound mind after that "education" so if you are trying to deny that then you are trying to deny absolute fact and one cannot deny absolute fact they can only be ignorant to absolute fact. You may want to go ask someone if what I explain is true but you perhaps do not know anyone who escaped the mind trap after they got the traditional education so you will only be asking people who are hallucinating like you are. What this means is you are on a raft in the ocean and everything comes down to you. No one in this universe can help you escape the mind trap you are in but you. You are factually in the mind trap because you got the traditional education. You have to get past that part because that is already establish as a fact, or it is impossible you are not in a mind trap, left brain bent, after you get the traditional education. You cannot change that absolute fact so you have to let go of trying to change that absolute fact. You sense time so that is proof you are in the mind trap. It is not important why you were put in the mind trap, it is only important you understand how to get out, and then you try to get out. One cannot cry over split milk. You're in the trap and that is split milk, that is the past and that is something you cannot change, so you have to focus on getting out of the trap. Now is where you are at, and that is under the left brain influence, mind trap. - 4:33:40 PM

Every tool can have unintended side effects.

6:41:46 PM – I have moments were I understand you are my friend and I have moments where I understand you are the adversary. I try to give you the benefit of the doubt but that is not wise to do that. I understand your track record of abuse, the left brain influenced containers. I was mentally abused because I was taught the education improperly and then I was showing symptoms of that abuse and I had to go through what the ancient texts call hell to get out of that mental place, the left brain influenced containers put me in. I do not want you to get the impression I think you know what you do because I understand you in fact are totally insane and are not capable of knowing what you do in the X state of mind. I cannot and will not trust a factually mentally insane person. What that means is you had the same mental abuse done to you that was done to me but I escaped it and you have not, so I cannot trust you. I write in diary format so you never ever get the impression I am talking to you because I no longer talk you, ever. If you met me in person and asked me a question I would answer but in my mind you are just an illusion now and I do not talk to illusions so my answer would be me talking to myself. You abused me too much. I am not angry or mad or upset because I am not capable of maintaining those emotions any longer. My emotions are at the normal level so I cannot become angry or bitter with you for more than a second relative to a clock, so I am just mindful to never talk to you. So I have this paradox in my mind, paradox is a right brain trait, that is I want to destroy you and help you at the exact same time. I want to wipe you out of existence and bring you back to life, sound mind, at the exact same time. There is no word in your feeble language that defines wanting to destroy and create at the exact same time. Your little written language invention works great as long as the person has their mind bent all the way to the left which is leaves one simpleminded and sequential in thoughts but it does not really pan out very well when the powerhouse, right brain, is active. You are convinced of all your little words. You believe if you can spell your little words properly it will prove to the universe you are not factually completely insane in your X state of mind. Your insanity factually was induced by learning how to spell all your little words properly and you insult beings who cannot spell all those words properly, as in children, with your spelling tests so you are factually beyond the description of sinister.

Your ability to spell words is not only not going to get you out of the mental trap you are in, your ability to spell words is one main reason you are in the mental trap you are in. You should attempt to be mindful I do not publish my words under fiction because they are not fiction. My words are not opinions. I leave opinions to the ones who do not have anything factually important to say. The rules of this plane of existence are simply this. People in civilization, left brain influenced containers have the right to mentally abuse children, knowingly or unknowingly, by administering this traditional education on that child, and the catch is if one of those children wakes up from that mental abuse, civilization is going to pay. That is not my opinion that is the rule of existence and that is an indication of how grave of a crime it is to veil right brain in a human being and leave that being mentally suffering in what is known in the ancient texts as hell.

T. C. (18) allegedly committed suicide by overdosing on anti-depressants

This could have been me. I had this accident because I took a bunch of anti-depressants to die. I write about that oft in my books because it's burned into my mind. I cannot become angry or bitter or grateful but none the less I am mindful of it. Your little traditional education bent my mind to the left and it almost killed me but the funny thing is it did not kill me. Relative to me that is the funniest thing in the universe and relative to civilization, the left influenced containers, that is Armageddon, psychologically speaking, so to speak, what have you, such and such. You wish, left brain influenced container, all of your laws and weapons and rules will protect you from me, right brain influence, but that only proves you are hallucinating to a degree I am unable to explain fully in infinite books. Perhaps my comments make you weird or afraid because you perhaps you assume I am anything like you. I am a child you have abused and now the worm has turned so civilization, left brain influenced containers, should be infinitely worried, infinitely stressed, and infinitely concerned to the point of cardiac arrest. I am, right brain influence, not here to start a cult I am strictly here on a vengeance mission. Civilization, left brain influenced containers, is worried about its money and so it is far too blind to understand one of the children it abused woke up. I , right brain influence, go out of my way to mention in my personal diary that civilization, left brain influenced containers, almost killed me but it fell short of the mark because of its mark. Civilization by improperly administering traditional education killed this little girl (T. C. (18) allegedly committed suicide by overdosing on anti-depressants) and it killed you mentally also, so you are perhaps infinitely blind to the fact what I suggest is reality. I am, right brain influence, a missile and the coordinates to the target has been entered and I am going full speed to the target, and there is not a dam thing you, left brain influenced container, can do, heaven can do, or hell can do, to stop me. That does not mean I am angry it simply means the coordinates have been entered. It would be a different situation if I did not have freedom of speech. It would be a different situation if civilization, left brain influenced containers, could do something to me that would make me do anything but laugh. Simply put I, right brain influence, woke up after having being veiled by traditional education and I am mindful civilization, left brain influenced containers, is doing the exact same thing to innocent children and so I, right brain influence, am going to incite Armageddon with my words on civilization, left brain influenced containers, psychologically speaking, so to speak, and then there will be none, such and such. It is not important if I win because in all reality I should be this [committed suicide by overdosing on anti-depressants]. I am mindful you perhaps just don't get it. - 7:32:21 PM

10:29:11 PM – The above comments are quite convincing to ones who are mentally unsound, left brain influenced containers. The old English Folk Rhyme "Sticks and stones will break my bones but words will never harm me." is perhaps beyond your mental ability to apply in your current X state of mind. You have been conditioned into such a neurotic state of mind you will act on words. You will harm someone because of words and you will harm yourself because of words. You will lock someone in jail because of words and thus you will lock yourself in jail because of words. You will beat children because of words because you were beaten as a child because of words. You will judge people because of their words because you are judged because of your words. You are simply afraid of words and that is a symptom of an unsound mind. In reality written languages are simply shapes arranged into a sequential fashion so they are in fact meaningless unless one has been conditioned to believe they have meaning. If I say "kill" you will think I am displeased and if I say "love" you will think I am pleased. You base your assumptions on the premise the words are real because you have been systematically conditioned mentally to believe everything you hear. You have been conditioned to believe this, sticks and stones will break my bones and I will die if someone says certain words. You are clinically a nervous wreck in your X state of mind. The traditional education has bent your mind so far to the left so you have little right brain intuition to the degree you can get the spirit of the words. What that means is all you have left is to believe every single word as an absolute. If someone says you are stupid you believe it because you believe the word stupid and so if anyone says you are stupid you believe them. If someone says you are wise, and I find it difficult they ever would in your unsound state of mind, you also believe that. The intuition and ambiguity of right brain allows a person to question the words so when traditional education veils the right brain they lose that ability and so they are stuck with not being able to question the words.

R. N. (17) committed suicide after being "cyber-bullied"
C. R. (14) committed suicide after being cyber-bullied

This is definitive proof people kill their self because of words. The deeper reality is these children were mentally bent to the left by traditional education so they were unable to question words spoken to them because right brain ambiguity and intuition was veiled. Deeper still this left brain conditioning turns up ones emotions to dangerous levels. What these two innocent children did is they heard words and believed the words and those words hurt their feelings because their feelings are turned up to dangerous levels by the left brain conditioning called traditional education. If these two innocent children did not have their right brain veiled they would have not been able to maintain a level of "sadness" if someone did say harsh words to them for more than a moment relative to a clock because right brain is going through thoughts so swiftly one is unable to maintain a set "emotional" mindset for very long as in minutes or less relative to a clock. The reason these children killed their self is because they were ashamed or embarrassed because they believed the words, because their right brain was veiled, so all they could do is believe the words and their left brain ponders sequentially and slowly in contrast to right brain so they maintained a state of shame long enough they decided to kill their self. This is known as depression or sadness but those emotions are not possible in any lasting duration when right brain is unveiled. A better way to look at it is when right brain is unveiled one has emotions on a fractional level and a fraction duration compared to ones who do not have right brain unveiled, ones who haven't applied the fear not remedy. I am trying to explain something and the words are not working. Think about having an emotion for 5 seconds and then you go back to no emotions. Think about laying down and being totally relaxed with nothing on your mind and that is how one is 99% of the time when they have right brain unveiled and once in a while they feel this emotion happy or sad or angry but they swiftly revert back to that relaxed state of mind, as in seconds relative to a clock. I call it neutral state of mind but some call it nirvana but what it really is, is sound mind, consciousness. Simply put I cancelled out the extreme left brain state of mind traditional education conditioned me into and no I am no longer a nervous wreck mentally.

If I summed up my state of mind over a one week period relative to a calendar I would say neutral and that goes for a 24 hour period relative to a clock.

The definition of the Nobel prize in literature is, one who can arrange words in a such a fashion to excite emotions. What that really means is they give out an award based on the fact civilization as a whole has extreme emotions because of the traditional education conditioning. I can scare you or make you happy or make you sad with my word arrangements, but you cannot do the same to me on the same level, so I can manipulate you with words but you are unable to manipulate me with words. I cannot stay up at night wondering what the world will say about what I write because right brain is pondering so fast I am quite certain it does not even acknowledge the world at all anymore. What is interesting is I use to be worried about what the world thinks about me. You believe the words because every single person you know believes the words, because every single person you know got traditional education and their mind is bent to the left. Simply put you based your reality on the assumptions of lunatics. You are still as you read this sentence assuming I am making harsh comments in my words but in absolute reality is am simply converting right brain, subconscious relative to you, thoughts into an infinitely flawed language. Another way to look at it is I have freedom of speech and right brain unveiled and it does not give a rats ass about anything a person who has an unsound mind thinks about what it says. My mind is indifferent to what the world thinks about what it writes. I am humbled to show you the path out of the place you have been thrown, but I will not wait for you because I am forging further up the mountain. - 11:34:57 PM

12/5/2009 12:50:00 AM – In the world of the sane, the ones with their minds bent left, there is a belief that if one commits suicide they will go to hell. What they are not aware of is their minds were bent to the left by the education and that is what hell is and the only way they will ever get out of hell is to commit mental suicide. Those who lose their life will preserve it. This "suicide belief" is an excellent example of the reverse world in action. Six billion people in the reverse world go around saying if you commit suicide you will go to hell and the only way one can escape hell, the place of suffering, and suffering is being in extreme left brain from the tree of knowledge, traditional education, is to commit mental suicide. The reverse world is so backwards the exact thing one has to do to get out of hell is the exact thing the reverse world says is the worst thing one can ever do. The blind are leading the blind away from the door out of hell. You do not ever have to worry about hell because you got the education and so you are in hell I assure you of that, and so the only chance you have ever to get out is to start thinking in reverse of how you think.

Those who lose their life will preserve it = commit mental suicide to get out of that mental hell you are in after the education. You perhaps see that comment as a lie, and because you see it as a lie you are in a universe of suffering. You will tell me you are not suffering because all you have known since you started to get the education conditioning is suffering. I can perhaps reach the ones who are downtrodden and poor in spirit because they are close to actually committing actual suicide but the ones who love the reverse world are pleased with suffering so they do not want to leave it. The suicidal people and depressed people do not like the suffering in hell so they are open minded and desire to leave hell, the left brain extreme state of mind. You do not have to defend the ones who put you in mental hell via the education although you wish to defend them. You perhaps wish to defend the ones, left brain influenced containers, who put you in mental hell because they are so great in number you cannot face them in your state of mind. Your emotions are turned up so high from being in the hell state of mind if you believed civilization mentally rapes children and you were one of them you would go into such rage, depression, anger and hate all at the same time you would perhaps end up harming yourself in some way, so you stay in your denial world because you cannot face harsh reality. One has to be in sound mind to face such harsh realities without harming their self. It is not what I suggest is false it is simply your mind is protecting you because harsh realities like that would destroy you in your state of mind, so your mind protects you and tells you some sequential based logic that make you say to yourself mentally "He is lying." and then you can go on with your life, which is suffering in mental hell. I am indifferent to how you feel because I am not in hell anymore. I do not know how you feel about what I say because I no longer feel what ones in hell feel, because I am no longer in hell. I escaped hell, accidentally, and I should just keep my mouth shut but I am a fool because I am going back into hell to try to bring my friends out but it is on my terms. I am not trying to bring you out of hell on your terms I am trying to bring you out of hell on my terms and many in hell see the way out of hell as dangerous so they are trapped in hell. The nature of hell means one is pleased to suffer so they cling to hell. You have had moments of depression, anger, hate, loss and so you know what suffering is but you believe those things are a part of life when in reality they are a symptom one is in hell. Perhaps you think you can suffer in hell in life and then you die, and can go to hell and suffer in hell. - 1:20:43 AM

8:56:15 AM – Kindness is universally thought to be a good thing relative to some. Hate is universally thought to be bad relative to some. Since all words are labels and all labels are relative to the observer, kindness and hate are not absolutes so they are essentially attempts to create separation. For example if someone says they are kind and they say another person is hateful, they are confused because by saying that they are not kind. A person may perceive they are kind when they punish another person for exhibiting certain behavior but because proper or improper behavior is relative to the observer if the initial person is punishing someone for exhibiting what they perceive is improper behavior but it is not improper behavior they are really just hateful. If a person from civilization see's a female from a tribe that lives in the Amazon not wearing a top that person from civilization may suggest that female is evil or bad and perceive they are being kind or trying to correct that perceived evil behavior when in reality they are being hateful. Because all the words are labels and relative to the observer one can

23

believe they are being kind when they are really being hateful. One who is always kind will end up being hateful and one who is always hateful will end up being kind. The concept tough love means one is hateful in order to achieve kindness. One may send their child to bed without dinner because the child failed a test in school. One may spank that child if that child says a perceived cuss word. So that person is being hateful and kind at the exact same time relative to their perception. Because of this kindness is not real and hateful is not real because both are relative to the observer and thus are not absolutes.

I perceive I am kind to tell you the traditional education hinders the mind into an unsound and thus dangerous state but civilization, left brain influenced containers, will assume I am hateful because I am attacking an invention civilization only considers is kind to teach to children. The many years of sequential education does in fact alter the perception of a child drastically and thus alters a child's mind so that is not relative to the observer so that is what is called a fact. Relative to civilization that has been pushing this traditional education on every child they are not concerned about facts because that particular fact would mean they are in hot water. So traditional education is supposed to make one less ignorant but if a person became too wise that is bad. Governments want to make people wise but they do not want them to be so wise they understand government secrets. I am aware for example I cannot stay on track in these books. I cannot stay on topic. I skip around. Now relative to a person who is bent mentally to the left anything that is not sequential is crazy because a person mentally bend to the left is usually only capable of sequential thoughts because that is a trait of left brain. So you may perceive I cannot be wise because I cannot write sequentially in my thoughts oft. One has to understand proof when they see it. My right brain is unveiled so it's totally logical I should only be able to essentially write in random access thoughts because random access is a right brain trait. Right brain is not good at short term memory so I can start writing about something and within a few sentences I totally forget what I started writing about and I just go from one sentence to another. This is what the now is. It's the machine state.

The government has launch codes to weapons that can destroy the human race. The government is trusted and assumed to be wise because they are the keepers of launch codes of weapons that can destroy the human race. What are the chances this government is so trusted and so wise to have those launch codes but is ignorant about what traditional education does to the mind of a child if not taught properly? A public school is a school that teaches traditional education and is funded by the government via tax payers. So tax payers being ignorant about the mental effects of traditional education on the mind of children are actually harming their own children and others children because they enable the traditional education by paying taxes to encourage the traditional education.

A masochist is one who tends to invite and enjoy misery of any kind.

X = mind altering traditional education
Y = people who fund traditional education and got traditional education who did not apply the remedy

Z = mental suffering caused by traditional education
A = a child who has not been educated

X + A = Z
X + Y + A = Z
Y(Z) + A = Z

Y(Z) is suffering and by funding traditional education and encouraging children to get it there is more suffering. Not only are the children suffering mentally after the education the people who fund the education experience the suffering of the children so their suffering is increased. Not only are the (Y)'s suffering because they got the education they are also suffering because by funding the education for children they then have to watch the children suffer and that makes them suffer more.

C. R. (14) committed suicide after being cyber-bullied. The parents of this child paid tax money to fund the traditional education that mentally put their child in a state of mind, left bent, that caused their child to kill their self when someone said words to them because that child's emotions were turned up to dangerous level as a result of the traditional education. So the parents of said child are not only are suffering because they got the traditional education and did not apply the remedy they paid taxes to put their child in that suffering state of mind and when their child kill their self the parents had to suffer even more. So the parents did it to their self because they are no longer mentally viable, left brain bent, and are harming their self without even knowing it.

A masochist is one who tends to invite and enjoy misery of any kind.

The problem with this word masochist is the Y's do not know that is what they are doing. The Y's are masochists that are not aware they are masochists.

An insane person is considered legally incompetent or irresponsible because of a psychiatric disorder. One who has their mind bent to the left even 1% is factually mentally unsound and that is a psychiatric disorder but traditional education bents the mind to the left perhaps as much as 90% to the point right brain is nothing but a subconscious aspect.

Another definition of insane is a person that shows a complete lack of reason or foresight.

(Y) funds an invention called traditional education that actually harms the sound mind of a child and is not aware of it at all to the degree Y perceives it is helping children when in fact it is mentally harming children and that is the definition of and insane person, a person that shows a complete lack of reason or foresight. This is exactly why Jesus said [Like 23:34 ; for they know not what they do.]
Only insane people and possessed people know not what they do.

Timothy leaned to the, your insane side [2 Timothy 1:7 For God hath not given us the spirit of fear; but .. of a sound mind.]

I am not suggesting you are insane because you were born insane I am suggesting you got traditional education and that made you insane. What that means is you were a child and not insane and then civilization, which all got the traditional education, and in turn are insane, saw you and because you were sane they saw sanity as insanity, so they "fixed" you, with the traditional education, and now you are insane. You can function as long as your scale of functioning is contrasted with insane people.

A lunatic is one considered thoughtless, reckless and one affected by a psychiatric disorder.

This, $X + Y + A = Z$ and this $Y(Z) + A = Z$ = reckless and thoughtless.

"A casual stroll through the lunatic asylum shows that faith does not prove anything."
Friedrich Nietzsche

[lunatic asylum] This wise being, right brain influenced container, sound minded container, was referring to civilization, left brain containers, and called it a lunatic asylum. He also wrote a book called Anti-Christ. He argued that Buddhism was not as damaging so to speak as western religions because Buddhism avoided the concept of God. This comment God is relative to what ones definition of God is. I understand God is right brain, so I am pleased with God, and I am not ashamed of God, and I am pleased with the complexity and intuition and paradox and the unnamable power of God.

I write books and attack the ones who hate God, the left brain containers, and I know they hate God because they push this invention called traditional education on innocent children and do not teach it properly so the education veils God in those children so those children become lunatics and insane, like the ones who push the traditional education on the children are lunatics and insane. I don't believe in the God you believe in because the God you believe in tells you it is okay to veil God, right brain, the God image, in innocent children. We have conflicting points of view and I can make quite a convincing argument relative to anyone on this planet. All you have to do is come up with a more convincing argument than I have, and I will follow you. The only problem with that is I do not listen to you or talk to you anymore so first you are going to have to convince me to listen and talk to you. The problem with that is I am mindful to never listen or talk to you again.

The story goes that Nietzsche had a nervous breakdown because he saw one of the lunatics beating a horse and he ran and grabbed the neck of the horse to protect the horse from the lunatic, left brain influenced container. His heightened awareness was getting the better of him towards the end. This is typical of some saints also. It all comes back to the saying "Ignorance is bliss". Bliss is spiritual joy and if you claim you have spiritual joy you are either a liar or ignorant to the fact civilization bends innocent children minds to the left and puts them in mental hell, the place of suffering. I am in neutral so I certainly will never have a nervous breakdown. I defeated my fear of death so I certainly have no reason to be nervous because I got that eventuality out of the way. I don't get nervous around lunatics or because of the deeds of clinical lunatics.

In his Book Anti-Christ, Nietzsche wrote this in the preface. "... must be honest in intellectual matters to the point of harshness to so much as endure my seriousness, my passion." He is trying to apologize for his book.

In my fourth book I started the book by saying this "This is a legal notice and warning.

This book is the diary of a being that was ripped mentally from a physical based state of mind, to an unknown state of mind as a result of an accident."

Ones who unveil right brain are fully aware they are dealing with lunatics called civilization, left brain influenced containers, because all of civilization got the education and their minds are bent to the left so they are unsound in mind and that is what a lunatic is. I was apologizing for the fact I negated the mental rape that happened to me as a child at the hands of civilization with that warning. I was defending the ones who mentally raped me and that is a common reaction to one who has been raped. They perceive it is their fault they were raped. I went through that stage for several volumes but as I warmed up I started to see clearly and now I not only do not apologize for my words, now I go out of my way to attack the ones, left brain influenced containers, who mentally raped me. I no longer run from mental rapists of innocent children, I am at the stage I run at them.

Nietzsche was a good example of what can happen if one gets stuck half way up the mountain. Meditation or what is known in the west as prayer, relative to the comment always remain in a state of prayer, it is a method to escape the left brain mental suffering trap, hell.

Essentially the logic behind mediation or prayer is one tries to avoid the emotions that arise in the mind or denies the emotions that arise in the mind. That is relative to this comment.

[Mark 8:34 And when he had called the people unto him with his disciples also, he said unto them, Whosoever will come after me, let him deny himself, and take up his cross, and follow me.]

[let him deny himself]

Himself being one who gets the traditional education which makes one a left brain influenced container, so their mind is unsound so in order to negate that they have to deny their self and meditation/prayer is simply denying ones thoughts in that state of mind. Once one escapes the mind trap there is no reason to meditate so ones who are mediating simply have not escaped the mind trap yet.

If one is sitting there with their eyes closed and a thought of greed or lust or desire enters their mind and they do not act on it and lets it pass they deny their self or their thoughts in that unsound state of mind and if one does it long enough they eventually silence those thoughts. The key is they have to do it long enough. The problem with that is, going from unsound mind to completely unveiling right brain and returning to sound mind has many stages. There are simply stages you do not want to get stuck at, and that is why this wise being, a right brain influenced container, as well as all the ancient texts explained the absolute fastest way to get through those stages.

[Luke 17:33 ; and whosoever shall lose his life shall preserve it.]

This method among other methods, the Abraham and Isaac method, the Submit method and the John the Baptist method are simply going to the extreme of [let him deny himself]. Simply put if you decide you want to wake up and return to sound mind you do it the full measure and that means you defeat your fear of death and that means all the fear will leave. If you mess around and try the slow routes, like meditation you may get stuck in an unwanted stage. For example the right brain has lots of ambiguity, creativity, intuition (heightened awareness) and once one starts unveiling the right brain if they only unveil it partially relative to how veiled it is after the education, they may get stuck with the strong emotions and have right brain unveiled a bit, and that may lead to one having heightened awareness but still having the strong emotions, and then one may have a nervous breakdown. The point is, waking up is a ride one wants to get over with swiftly and the only way to get it over with swiftly is to defeat the greatest fear and that is fear of death. You have nothing to fear if you do not fear death when your hypothalamus tells you the shadow of death is near, and so after that is accomplished you are unable to be nervous about anything ever again. So down through history there are one's who woke up part of the way, and they stuck out, and then there are ones who woke up all the way and they really stuck out.

About a month after you apply the defeat ones fear of death remedy the right brain will unveil. It is so powerful you will be mentally paralyzed for about two months. Your mind is conditioned to sequential left brain thought patterns and when you apply this remedy and right brain unveils your mind will have to adjust to going from slothful thoughts to light speed thoughts. You are now in a car with one piston and after the remedy you will wake up with a car with 18 pistons and so you are going to have to learn everything over again relative to the mental power you have now. This is what is known in the ancient texts as the resurrection. You are going to be mentally resurrected from slothful mental death. After two months you will notice the right brain traits starting to kick in. Your creativity is going to be off the scale. Your intuition (heightened awareness) is going to be off the scale. Your ambiguity or doubt is going to be off the scale and your pattern detection is going to be off the scale. Your feeling thorough vision and telepathy are simply going to be the intuition aspect and that will seem very strange at first. You will essentially be getting accustomed to consciousness. As long as you apply the fear not remedy , defeat your fear of death, all you have to do is go with the flow because you are going up to the top of the mountain in a chariot, psychologically speaking. After the remedy is applied you think for yourself from then on out and that is an indication right brain is the only teacher you need from then on out. There are stages early on of paranoia caused by all the ambiguity but you are in a chariot so that stage passes swiftly. You will start getting the spirit of things you see and read and so your ability to write and read will be altered. You are going to be paranoid also about going back to how you were. You are going to be mindfully concerned about going back because you will be so pleased with how things are after right brain is unveiled, so you will be paranoid about losing these newly unleashed powers. You will experience the power of right brain and gain all these great aspects of heightened awareness and think you have discovered something new or gained something new but in reality all you have done is unveiled what you always had so you cannot lose it because you always had it, it was just veiled by the education. So you are not gaining something as much as you are turning something on that was turned off and once it is turned back on it cannot be turned off. As a child your mind was not mature or developed and at the age of six or less you started all this sequential conditioning called traditional education and so your mind was bent to the left before it was even developed. So now you are an adult and your mind is developed and once you unveil right brain it is permanent and nothing will make it go back to being veiled because, its complex, but right brain won't allow you to veil it again. Some I speak with are paranoid about using written language at all for fear they may go back but I am actually writing so much to prove to myself I cannot go back even if I use written language oft. For that reason alone I understand I am not against written language or math or traditional education because it is a good tool, my point is these tools have factually devastating mental side effects if not applied properly on an innocent child's mind that is not even developed. It's a great paradox.

Traditional education is good

Traditional education is bad.

I am not going to wake up tomorrow and my hypothalamus is going to cloud my mind with fear because I defeated my fear of death accidentally so if I write a lot my hypothalamus may want to start giving false strong signals of fear but the amygdala has memories about fear and so it tells the hypothalamus," This guy didn't run like a scared dog when you gave him the death signal in that last suicide attempt" so hypothalamus cannot start its false fear signals ever again so there is no way my mind cannot go back.

So this remedy [Luke 17:33 ; and whosoever shall lose his life shall preserve it.] is a onetime mental exercise, and it takes one second to accomplish in the right situation, and then everything is fixed mentally or the educations bad mental side effects are negated. That is what the tragedy is about all of this. For 5000 years mankind has been killing each other over a mental remedy that can be applied in one second and then everything is fine with our species mentally. Everything relative to the entire history of mankind is relative to ones who get the education and do not apply the remedy to negate it bad mental side effects, the left brain influenced containers, and ones who do apply the remedy to negate it bad mental side effects, right brain influenced containers, and all of that is relative to the fact we could just educate the children orally until their minds are developed and then they can figure out all the education they "missed" in about a year or less and be Einstein's mentally and the not have to apply the remedy. Vanity is simply going through a thousand tormenting steps when you only had to go through one painless step. - 11:53:26 AM

10:17:37 PM – This comment is relative to the fact once the remedy is applied it cannot be broken or unapplied or you cannot go back to the unsound state of mind.

[Hebrews 6:2 Of the doctrine of baptisms, and of laying on of hands, and of resurrection of the dead, and of eternal judgment.

Hebrews 6:3 And this will we do, if God permit.

Hebrews 6:4 For it is impossible for those who were once enlightened, and have tasted of the heavenly gift, and were made partakers of the Holy Ghost,

Hebrews 6:5 And have tasted the good word of God, and the powers of the world to come,

Hebrews 6:6 If they shall fall away, to renew them again unto repentance; seeing they crucify to themselves the Son of God afresh, and put him to an open shame.]

The spirit of these words is saying once you apply the remedy and taste the right brain you cannot go back, or it will not allow you to go back. So relative to this time frame, baptism was a popular method to apply the remedy. One could look at it like John the Baptist was the one who came up with the Baptism method. He perfected it. It is very similar to the method Abraham used in principle. Abraham bound someone and placed them on alter and held a knife over them and that person believed he was going to kill them and they did not run, so they feared not. So John dunked someone under water and held them there and when that person thought they were going to drown they did not fight it so they let go mentally so they submitted, and that is in principle what the Abraham and Isaac remedy is. The complexity here is one conditioned into the X state of mind after the education has to literally seek to die relative to their point of view and then not fight when they perceive death is upon them. That is what is required to escape the mind trap fully, so one can perhaps understand how deep they have fallen mentally after they get all this sequential education as a child.

[and of resurrection of the dead] This comment is not relative to just one person being resurrected from the dead. It is relative to a doctrine of being resurrected from the dead. One is conditioned into X state of mind from traditional education, so their mind is bent to the left and they are what is known relative to that time period as the dead, so they apply the remedy and they are resurrected and that means they are returned to sound mind, unveil right brain, and they are the quick.

[1 Corinthians 15:42 So also is the resurrection of the dead. It is sown in corruption; it is raised in incorruption:]

[sown in corruption] simply means one gets the traditional education essentially forced on them by civilization so corruption would be civilization, the left brain influenced containers.

[it is raised in incorruption:] This comment is relative to a few other comments, the phoenix rising from the ashes and, one has to go through hell to get to heaven(unveil right brain.)

[Acts 17:32 And when they heard of the resurrection of the dead, some mocked: and others said, We will hear thee again of this matter.]

On one hand they could have perhaps used better wording than resurrect the dead because telling unsound minded beings one can resurrect the dead is asking for trouble, but on the other hand right brain is so powerful once one unveils it they will only be able to explain, mentally before they unveiled right brain they were essential dead mentally in contrast.

[some mocked] It is okay if you mock the spirit of what I suggest. I am not going to find fault with you if you mock the spirit of what I suggest. I am mindful you were a child and you were educated by traditional means as I was and that means your mind was bent to the left and the bending is so subtle it is simply not your fault. You were a child and beings you trusted to watch over you led you to learn a mind altering invention and it altered your mind but they also got the mind altering invention so they knew not what they were doing so I find no fault with them. Traditional education is factually a tool that if not taught properly it has unintended mental consequences that are devastating. Ones who mock that are proof of how devastating the mental consequences are. It is a worldwide mental drowning. The truth will set you free because if you can get to the stage you understand cause and effect relationships relative to this traditional education on the mind, then you may ask the next question which is "How do I negate these unwanted mental side effects caused by years of sequential left brain education?"

[John 11:25 Jesus said unto her, I am the resurrection, and the life: he that believeth in me, though he were dead, yet shall he live:]

[Mark 6:14 And king Herod heard of him; (for his name was spread abroad:) and he said, That John the Baptist was risen from the dead, and therefore mighty works do shew forth themselves in him.]

[[Jesus said unto her, I am the resurrection]

[That John the Baptist was risen from the dead]

[Psalms 73:22 So foolish was I, and ignorant: I was as a beast before thee.]]
= Ones who were conditioned into the unsound left brain state of mind by the written language and then they applied the remedy, fear not remedy etc, and woke up or regained sound mind, returned to being right brain influenced containers as they were as children, so they return to being children of god.

Who raised Jesus from the dead or woke Jesus up or assisted Jesus to break the left brain state of mind caused by the written language?

[Mark 1:9 And it came to pass in those days, that Jesus came from Nazareth of Galilee, and was baptized of John in Jordan.

Mark 1:10 And straightway coming up out of the water, he saw the heavens opened, and the Spirit like a dove descending upon him:

Mark 1:11 And there came a voice from heaven, saying, Thou art my beloved Son, in whom I am well pleased.

Mark 1:12 And immediately the Spirit driveth him into the wilderness.]

[Jesus came from Nazareth of Galilee, and was baptized of John in Jordan.] John the Baptist using the method to wake people up, being under the influence of right brain, raised Jesus from the dead using his baptism technique.

What Happened after John applied his remedy method on Jesus?

[And straightway coming up out of the water, he saw the heavens opened] [he saw the heavens opened] = the mind open up, the mind returned to sound mind, right brain unveiled.

John the Baptist knew he went the full measure with Jesus and what the means is Jesus defeated his fear of death to the extreme using his baptism method so John said. [Thou art my beloved Son, in whom I am well pleased.]

So John the Baptist, being under the influence of right brain, is the big fish, the Master , the Lord relative to the new testament in that respect.

This is what a left brain influence container will perhaps be thinking about the above comments I have suggested.

[Matthew 9:3 And, behold, certain of the scribes said within themselves, This man blasphemeth.]

[Thou art my beloved Son, in whom I am well pleased.] is simply suggesting John the Baptist knew Jesus was going to be a great spokesman for the cause, the cause being, explaining to people the unwanted side effects of the traditional education and also being able to explain how others could apply the remedy if they got the traditional education. Jesus did not suggest baptism he explained the remedy as "deny ones self" and "those who lose their life will preserve it." So the spirit, the right brain, kept improving its explanation of the remedy, in all of these beings. The remedy just got easier and easier to explain so to speak.

John the Baptist said something along the lines of: Jesus, who comes after me is greater than me and that is simply an indication on one hand John the Baptist was infinitely humble and on the other hand Jesus came from civilization so people perhaps could relate better to him than perhaps John the Baptist who was in the wilderness. John the Baptist lived in a cave in the wilderness so he was not of civilization so to speak any longer.

This [and was baptized of John in Jordan.] is suggesting John the Baptist was the teacher of Jesus not the other way around but John was under the influence of right brain so in that respect it was not John at all, it was right brain.

[And immediately the Spirit driveth him into the wilderness.]This comment is relative to intuition, a right brain trait, or heightened awareness. The reverse of civilization is the wilderness. Think about Moses, he freed the people and they returned to the wilderness. Abraham and Lot did not burn down the wilderness they burned down the cities of civilization, the cities of the left brain influenced containers.

[Genesis 19:13 For we will destroy this place, because the cry of them is waxen great before the face of the LORD; and the LORD hath sent us to destroy it.] [For we will destroy this place and the LORD hath sent us to destroy it] "We" and "(Us)" is Abraham and Lot and their armies. They were Generals of the right brain influenced containers. So in that respect they were not Abraham and Lot they were spokesman for right brain, they were compelled by right brain.

Jesus already knew the minute he applied the remedy what would happen to him eventually at the hands of civilization, the left brain influenced containers,

32

because the right brain can figure out the end conclusion instantly because it uses random access thoughts and intuition. Simply put he woke up so well after John assisted him with remedy, he knew he was going to assist others to wake up and civilization frowns on one's who try to wake its slaves up. To clarify, left brain hates right brain, it is jealous of right brain because right brain is the superior of the two aspects and so it see's right brain as bad because it sees itself as good. This is not about people as much as it is about this battle of the hemispheres, left and right brain. Left brain knows in a 50/50 harmony it plays second fiddle to right brain and it hates that so it wants to be by itself ort veil right brain to a subconscious aspect because it knows in 50/50 mental harmony right brain gets all the glory, or influence in a being. Again, this is not about people as much as it is about the battle of the hemispheres, they are minds unto their self beyond the people they dwell in. I am not Todd as much as I am a right brain influenced container, by accident. What I write is a symptom of right brain influence not a symptom of the fact my name is Todd.

Let's talk about doom. [Mark 6:14 And king Herod heard of him; (for his name was spread abroad:) and he said, That John the Baptist was risen from the dead, and therefore mighty works do shew forth themselves in him.]

King Herod is the powers that be relative to civilization, a power with left brain influence. The government's, which are the foundation of civilization, left brain influence. I will clarify what this Mark 6:14 is saying. The powers that be in civilization heard that John the Baptist woke up from the slumber traditional education put him in mentally and they wanted his head on a platter because he was very good at waking up others using his Baptism method. A deeper reality is left brain saw right brain broke free of its slumber and left brain wanted it dead. This is what the battle of the minds is all about. One has to understand the position the ones who wake up put civilization, the powers that be in.

Civilization, the governments only have two choices.

A. They can come out and tell everyone in civilization their traditional education does hinder the mind and make one slothful in thoughts and very afraid and then the people in civilization will need to be compensated and will never trust civilization, the governments again.

B. Kill the one who wakes up because if they do not he will spread the word and wake everyone up.

This is not an indication of how intelligent John the Baptist was or any of these being were, it is factually an indication how intelligent and powerful right brain is when unveiled and also an indication how right brain does not take to being veiled kindly. All that civilization, the government, the control structure can do is kill the one who unveils right brain the full measure because if they do not that being will wake every single person up out of the slumber the traditional education conditioning put them in and the taskmaster, civilizations power structure, will lose all of its slaves. Again the deeper reality is, left brain influenced containers see right brain influenced containers and want to kill them because at 50/50 mental harmony the left brain is the weaker of the two aspects so it is always relegated to #2 and it is jealous of the powerhouse house right brain. It is along the lines of sibling rivalry on a mind scale. The mind invented written language and this bent the mind to the left and left brain got a taste of power and right brain was relegated to a subconscious aspect and left brain does not want to go back to 50/50 mindset because it will be #2, so in that respect left brain is drunk with its new found power and will not give it up. Right brain cannot help it has complexity, intuition etc so right brain is like the better of the two aspects and that drives left brain to jealousy. So our minds are so powerful they are in a battle and the people, are not even involved they are just containers of these two aspects of mind who are in a battle. Humans are pawns in this mind battle that is taking place between our two hemispheres and that battle has been going on for 5000 years or more. It is not the people it is our minds are so powerful they are unto their self in a battle. Left brain can't survive by itself, that's why there are so many people suffering, but it also does not want to go back to 50% because then right brain gets all the glory and it hates that prospect. So people are reduced to containers of these mind aspects that are in a battle. Our minds are too powerful is one way to look at it.

[Mark 1: 14 Now after that John was put in prison, Jesus came into Galilee, preaching the gospel of the kingdom of God,]
[preaching the gospel of the kingdom of God,] All this is saying is John the Baptist was put into prison because he woke up from the conditioning and he was very adept at waking up others and civilization had to kill him or he would have freed the minds of everyone in civilization, he would have woken them all up. One cannot take or threaten to take power from a control freak, left brain, and expect the control freak to allow it. Civilization, left brain influenced containers, is the cult of the serpent and it uses its Trojan horse called traditional education to mentally put people to sleep, veil their right brain, knowingly or unknowingly, and all these ancient texts are talking about is that, and the remedy to escape that mental slumber the traditional education puts them in. I am not trying to force you to wake up, I am telling you civilization, the powers that be, does not want you to wake up, or they would not have put you to sleep to begin with unless they are insane and do not know they are putting people to sleep. I have no credentials relative to civilization, and relative to civilization I am the least among civilization. Relative to civilization there is no reason in the universe you should believe the spirit of what I suggest, so you are going to have to try your hardest to use your intuition. All I can say is, if the spirit of what I suggest was not true, I would not tell you it is true. - 11:42:52 AM

12/6/2009 5:15:59 AM — [1 Samuel 17:4 And there went out a champion out of the camp of the Philistines, named Goliath, of Gath, whose height was six cubits and a span.]
A philistine is simply a person who gets the education and does not apply the remedy. The camp of the philistines is simply civilization, left brain influenced.

[1 Samuel 17:23 And as he talked with them, behold, there came up the champion, the Philistine of Gath, Goliath by name, out of the armies of the Philistines, and spake according to the same words: and David heard them.]

[out of the armies of the Philistines] denotes civilization, left brain influenced containers, not only has many minions but also has vast standing armies. Civilization has many weapons because it cannot defeat anyone with its mind because its right brain is veiled from the education so it has to rely on weapons and vast armies. This is relative to the grains in the sea. This is relative to "even now there are many anti-Christ" in revelations. There are always great numbers of them because civilization pushes the traditional education on their own children and their own children push it on their children, their first born. If one plays around with something that can alter their mind and perception, and they are not even aware of it, it is going to alter their mind and perception. One has to keep in mind the time period of this event. At this time period the ones who pushed the education and did not apply the remedy were not as great in number as the time period of the New Testament.

Abraham and Lot burned down the cities and then Moses could not do that because civilizations, left brain numbers were too great so he just attacked the cities until the cities let the people go and then in the New Testament there was no chance to even attack the cities with any chance of a victory so it was an underground movement. Today Civilization does not even mention that there may be unwanted mental side effects after years of this sequential based education, traditional education that would affect the undeveloped mind of a child. That is all you perhaps ever need to know about the powers that be, the left brain influenced containers, relative to civilization.

The meaning of David and Goliath is that David applied the fear not remedy and had God, right brain, on his side and so he did not need an army because he has the powerhouse on his side. A deeper meaning is that one who applies the remedy regains a sound mind and they can slay the entire cult of civilization with their words. Deeper still is the left brain only see's right brain as bad. Right brain is okay with left brain being at 50% but that is because at 50% right brain is the brain influence. So in one respect one can have sympathy for what left brain is doing. Cain and Able are the first offspring of Adam and eve and Cain is the left brain and it is jealous of its brother able so it kills its brother Able, right brain, so Cain veils right brain. The name Cain is translated as the evil one, but in reality it is just a child that is jealous of its more powerful brother, right brain. Left brain found a way to dominate the mind and veil right brain and it does not want to give it up because if it allows right brain to be unveiled left brain will be second fiddle. That reality for left brain will never change so left brain is a troubled child so to speak. Some human beings can sing better than other human beings so sometimes human beings are jealous of the other human beings and that is what this battle is but on a mental level. Human beings are either left brain influenced, unsound mind, or right brain influenced, sound mind, and so relative to that they are nothing but fruits of the influence they are controlled by. - 5:49:55 AM

"You shall leave everything you love most: this is the arrow that the bow of exile shoots first. You are to know the bitter taste of others' bread, how salty it is, and know how hard a path it is for one who goes ascending and descending others' stairs."

Contrast this comment : [You shall leave everything you love most] with this commentary.
[Matthew 16:24 Then said Jesus unto his disciples, If any man will come after me, let him deny himself, and take up his cross, and follow me.]
[let him deny himself] = [You shall leave everything you love most]
This is relative to a concept about minimalism and detachment. One has to be mindful there are two worlds happening mentally; the ones who wakeup, and the ones yet to wake up from the education induced neurosis. A person who applies the fear not remedy etc, is not about minimalism and detachment. One does not wake up so they can bask in their own glory they are compelled to spread the light around so to speak. "This little light of mine I'm going to let it shine." These wise beings in these ancient texts for example did not go hide after they applied the remedy because hide denotes fear.
[Genesis 3:10 And he said, I heard thy voice in the garden, and I was afraid, because I was naked; and I hid myself.]
[hid] in this comment denotes after eating off the tree of knowledge he hid because he was [and I was afraid]. Dante was not a poet he was just a well disguised being who applied the remedy to some degree.
[this is the arrow that the bow of exile shoots first.] = What is an exile? Although he was exiled similar to how John of Revelations was exiled literally, exiled is the 9th circle of hell. This is the 9th circle of hell, treason, Dante spoke about [let him deny himself]. If one actually makes it through the 9th circle of hell, treason, they go to the next half of the "world" which is known as heaven, which means they unveil right brain.
Many do not make it through the 9th circle and they are what are known as suicides, or drug overdoses and things along those lines and many that do make it through are simply accidents. What I mean by accident is one in the reverse world does not see they are going through the 9th circle of hell, they see they are suffering and they cannot take the suffering any longer. They cannot take the extreme emotions caused by the left brain state of mind traditional education causes in them, and they want out. They hedge their bets and determine death might not have so much suffering.
This is very revealing and it relative to these comments.

[[You are to know the bitter taste of others' bread, how salty it is, and know how hard a path it is for one who goes ascending and descending others' stairs.]
[Jesus said unto her, I am the resurrection]
[That John the Baptist was risen from the dead]

[Psalms 73:22 So foolish was I, and ignorant: I was as a beast before thee.]] = Ones who were conditioned into the unsound left brain leaning state of mind by the written language and then they applied the remedy, fear not remedy etc, and woke up or regained sound mind.

This spirit of this section of words is simply saying, once one applies the remedy and unveils right brain they are fully aware of how much suffering they were in mentally, because right brain was veiled, and so they know how much suffering others are in, and they are fully aware of how difficult the path of the ones who have not applied there remedy yet, is.

[how hard a path it is for one who goes ascending and descending others' stairs.] This is a perfect explanation how one is in the unsound state of mind. They are up and down , up and down. One day they are depressed, one day they are happy and that happiness is only leading to more depression.

A good example is people who are exhibiting greed or lust or gluttony. When they get what they want, like control, money or drugs they are happy but all that really means is when they don't get it they are sad. They are happy as long as they get their little vice but if they do not get it they are depressed. They are not really happy or sad they are [ascending and descending others' stairs.] Ones who descend and ascend stairs are going to fall eventually. The first circle of hell is limbo and these are ones who are very delicate or ones who are capable of falling the farthest and the fastest.

This is why the ones who are poor in spirit or the down trodden are most valuable relative to reality world. For example, a person with lots of wealth and material things and has everything going for them relative to reverse world can in one day lose all that wealth and perceived security and go right to the 9th circle of hell, which is treason and cannot stand the heat in that circle so they tend to kill their self swiftly and absolutely. A person is a millionaire and the markets crash and they lose all their wealth and they kill their self because they perceive there is no point in living. Now the poor in spirit and downtrodden they are in the 9th circle or very close to it all their life so they are use to the heat so to speak. They do not tend to get flustered in the heat of the 9th circle, treason, like the rich man does.

[Acts 17:29 Forasmuch then as we are the offspring of God, we ought not to think that the Godhead is like unto gold, or silver, or stone, graven by art and man's device.]

One who has their right brain veiled tends to seek material things because their powerhouse cerebral aspect is veiled.[graven by art and man's device.] Graven art is written language and it is ' man+s device. Man in this comment is relative to [Genesis 11:5 And the LORD came down to see the city and the tower, which the children of men builded.] and the men who build the tower is relative to [Acts 4:11 This is the stone which was set at nought of you builders, which is become the head of the corner.]

Nought means nothing, and so this comment is saying the men of civilization who push the written education, the Saudacees, which are the scribes, [Matthew 23:27 Woe unto you, scribes and Pharisees, hypocrites! for ye are like unto whited sepulchres, which indeed appear beautiful outward, but are within full of dead men's bones, and of all uncleanness.]

The powers that be in civilization see the poor in spirit and the depressed as nothing but they are in fact much closer to escaping the mental hell they are put in than the rich in the reverse world will ever be, so they are the corners stones. So the meek and mild and humble in the reverse world are the poor and downtrodden and they are of greatest value in reality world.

This comment [ye are like unto whited sepulchres, which indeed appear beautiful outward, but are within full of dead men's bones, and of all uncleanness.] = [we ought not to think that the Godhead is like unto gold, or silver, or stone, graven by art and man's device.]

Material things are inanimate so they cannot be good or bad they just are. What these comments are saying is the trends or characteristics of civilization. One cannot fault a person who is materialistically wealthy because they got the education and their right brain veiled and so all they have is material things to attempt to feel worth from, but once they apply the remedy they will have cerebral wealth and all those material things will take a back seat. One will be a thinker and it will never occur to them to go carpet bag their friends to make some money because money isn't required to think. Money is only important to one who has been robbed of their ability to think. I am attempting to show you there is a lot more going on in the world than what your intuition is suggesting because intuition is a right brain trait and it has been veiled. I can read a few words from anyone and tell very swiftly if they applied the remedy to a degree or not and that is not because I am intelligent it is because this right aspect civilization continues to veil knowingly or unknowingly in children has such powerful pattern detection abilities I can only assume civilization knows not what it does. Civilization, left brain, shoots the good foot to save the other foot.- 2:10:24 PM

2:26:31 PM – A child can be taught the language strictly verbally. Sometimes a small child will ask a parent "What does that word mean?". The small child has right brain unveiled before they start traditional education so they are excellent mimics. All that child is doing is detecting patterns, spoken words in this case, and then repeating them. This is similar to what a parrot does. But traditional education is based on spelling and then one starts going down this sequential road or arranging letters in proper sequence, spelling, and arranging words in sentences in proper sequence, grammar. And then math is arranging numbers in proper sequence. And then history class is memorizing dates in proper sequence. And then there are all the rules to apply, to use written language and math, and that's all left brain traits and before you know it, traditional education is nothing but left brain conditioning. Even in kick ball there are rules and one has to run the bases in sequential order. There is nothing in traditional education that favors no rules and random access. Any child that breaks rules gets sent to the office and punished. Why isn't there a class where kids can say whatever they want and whatever is on their mind no matter what its is? Because they would break the rules with their words. What kind of control monstrosity are you, left brain, to punish children for speaking the thoughts in their minds? Rules are a left brain trait and right brain hates rules, it effects right brain pattern detection.- 2:36:48 PM

2:43:18 PM – How can anyone argue that even favoring left brain 1% and thus veiling right brain 1% is proper? I understand the traditional education leaves the mind at about 90% left brain and 10% right brain. How can a sane human being argue that is proper? How can any human being find fault with a child or a person who's mind has been molded so they have 90% left brain and 10% right brain inputs?
Only in a lunatic asylum would a person argue this mind ratio is proper and only the greatest lunatic would argue it is good to put a mind in that state and only a sinister would argue everyone should get that mind ratio. - 2:48:38 PM

3:02:13 PM – Civilization makes all these psychological medicines to treat mental illness but they never understand the mental illnesses like depression etc are symptoms of the traditional education is veiling the right brain. So civilization is never addressing problems it is addressing symptoms of the main problem. Because of this they can never fix the problem because they are bogged down addressing symptoms of the problem. The ones who get lots of the traditional education are the "leaders" of the ones who didn't get as much but both have their right brain veiled so it is just a funny farm of folly. You take a thousand blind people and cram them into a room and put grease on the floor and watch the action. Civilization has to grow more food because the education alters the perception so people are always hungry and need three huge meals a day just to maintain enough energy to remain mentally blind. I am not just complaining I am in fact offering a solution but I have no credentials relative to lunatic asylum world so I will just be brushed under the carpet because I am the stone, the stone cutter threw away. It is better to avoid putting a person in this mental situation, extreme left brain state of mind. It is better to educate children orally until they are of mature mind and then they can learn the written aspect of education swiftly because right brain will not veiled. That is utopia ideals but lunatic asylum world is pretty far from utopia. Lunatic asylum world prefers to create all these symptoms because they will not adjust the education methods and then they spend all their efforts trying to plug all the symptoms that arise when in reality all they have to do is adjust the education methods and all those symptoms will evaporate. I am not dealing with reasonable sound minded people I am dealing with lunatics with no reasoning abilities.
Utopia education would use the same school buildings as there are now except no textbooks, no chalk board, no tests, no homework ,nothing but verbal education. Now lunatic asylum world will argue that education won't make the children suffer enough. Lunatic asylum world simply does not understand as long as they keep that child's right brain unveiled until their mind matures, that child will learn infinitely more and infinitely faster than any human being on the planet will learn, who has their right veiled by traditional education. I am aware of what you are aware of, so we can avoid that topic. - 3:25:54 PM

5:18:21 PM –

In Aberdeen the rain was light
   I caught a glimpse of certain height
   The water passed upon that stone
I rested on but never owned.

- 5:22:25 PM

11:26:21 PM – There are some things one can do to prepare for applying the remedy. After the education one's mind is bent to the left so they see things are parts and because of this one tends to see the words as absolutes such as good and bad. In order to start conditioning the mind so right brain can be unveiled one wants to start using non absolutes relative to words. What these non absolute words are really doing mentally is helping one do this [let him deny himself] and that comment is relative to submit and also fear not, it a fear conditioning aspect using these non absolute words. Another way to look at it is self humiliation. So one's self is this left mind bent state of mind and one wants to start denying it and mental humiliation will start to free it up or let it go. Non absolute words are maybe and perhaps. If one wants to go to an extreme they start every sentence spoken or written with perhaps and ending in perhaps. This serves a few purposes. One will notice people will insult them for doing this and that is a form of humiliation and also using perhaps at the beginning and end of each sentence will mean one is never saying anything. Perhaps I am saying something perhaps. These words work when a person is mentally bent to the left, after the education, because they believe the words. The psychology is the left brain see's parts and thus absolutes and so perhaps is not an absolute so it is denying one's self, the left brain. Ones in the X state of mind likes to have definitive answers. Yes or no, good or bad, black or white, so using these non absolute words is slowly starting to condition the mind towards right brain. When one does not want to use the word perhaps and maybe that's when they should the most. Use these words when you're around friends and in conversation as much as you can and you will notice the people you speak to will start to insult you and become angry when you use perhaps too often. Freud said, Neurosis is the inability to tolerate ambiguity, and perhaps suggests doubt. You are not saying perhaps for anyone's benefit but your own and you will start to notice people will try to manipulate you for using perhaps too often. You are going to start to detect this bias against ambiguity and thus right brain by using these words. You are going to become and experimenter. You have to understand there are six billion people on this planet with their minds bent to the left and they do not take kindly to right brain aspects, complexity, paradox and ambiguity. The sooner you start looking at them as subjects to observe and experiment on by taking note of how they act based on what you say the sooner you will not let them manipulate you. If they do not want to unveil their right brain that is their business but avoid allowing them to make your decisions for you based on peer pressure or insults. They will say "You sound stupid because you say perhaps so much so stop it because you are bugging me." You ignore that and you say perhaps even more and then they may become very angry. You keep in mind what Freud said, Neurosis is the inability to tolerate ambiguity. They hate right brain, ambiguity is a right brain trait, ambiguity is doubt and the word perhaps is a doubt word. This

41

exercise is all relative to this comment [let him deny himself]. You are simply going to get accustomed to humiliation and you are going to try your best to look at everything as an experiment. When you do not want to say perhaps that is the most opportune time to say it. This is the basics to start favoring your right brain. You did not get yourself into this left brain bent, X state of mind, but only you can get yourself out so you get use to looking at people as illusions and this way when they insult you for saying perhaps to much it will not bother you because illusions cannot affect you with sounds or words. - 11:51:19 PM

12/7/2009 12:40:25 AM –
Acute Stress Disorder – This disorder is the result of a traumatic event; a person who experiences an event that involves death or serious injury and also is relative to intense fear or horror.
One who is in X state of mind, their mind bent to the left, has all their emotions turned up and also the emotions are long lasting relative to one who unveils right brain. The cause of this disorder is the persons mind is bent to the left as a result of the many years of sequential education. When right brain is unveiled a memory which is what this condition is relative to has its time stamps and also emotions stripped from it. A person in X state of mind relives this event over and over and that memory has the emotion stage on it and so it is like it is happening right then. This is indicative of a symptom of an unsound state of mind and in this case the X state of mind. This disorder is essentially PTSD and the main factor here is right brain when unveiled ponders so swiftly and removes the emotions stamps and time stamps from the memory so it is not even possible to ever achieve this disorder when right brain is unveiled. On top of that the fear is gone from the mind when right brain is unveiled, slight sensations of fear are possible but not more than a couple of seconds or a sensation of fear and this disorder denotes long period of fear relative to a clock. The left brain is relative to sequential thoughts and that is relative to sloth which means one can be stuck in a state of mind for long periods relative to a calendar but right brain is not only swift in going from one thought state to another but it is also random access. It would be best described as hyper manic/depressive with neutral being the dominate state of mind. One can have shades of happiness then depression but always go back to neutral all in about in as short of time as seconds relative to a clock. This is what the random access aspect is all about relative to emotions. The point is no emotional state can be maintained with right brain unveiled so the average emotional state is neutral.

Adjustment Disorders:
This disorder is simply a person who is a hyper nervous wreck. Anyone with their mind bent to the left is a nervous wreck in contrast to one who unveils right brain but this type of person tends to have lots of anxiety and that over time creates depression. Both of these emotions are impossible to maintain when right brain is unveiled so this disorder is simply a symptom of a slothful thought process and a sequential thought process caused by traditional education being taught improperly. The main difference in a person getting over anxiety and

depression relative to one being in bent left state of mind and one who unveils right brain is years compared to minutes. This is relative to the random access thought patterns and also the speed in thought patterns. One could be in this state for years and years when their mind is bent to the left and when right brain is unveiled they could not maintain this state of mind for more than a minute and that is an indication of how powerful right brain is when unveiled. Once the person gets the years of sequential educational and their mind bends to the left the person emotionally collapses. The emotions are turned up so high caused by the amygdala and hypothalamus and cerebral cortex not functioning properly in the left bend state of mind. One can only have emotional disorders when the mind is bent to the left, when the processing powerhouse right brain is veiled. One is simply going to get unsound emotional fruits from an unsound mind and the core problem is the education bends the mind to the left in the child before that's child's mind even develops. These disorders are not disorders they are symptoms of a mind in disorder or a mind that is unsound as a result of years of sequential left brain traditional education.

I cannot say it any better than this [Genesis 2:17 But of the tree of the knowledge of good and evil, thou shalt not eat of it: for in the day that thou eatest thereof thou shalt surely die.] and die in this case is one becomes emotionally unsound or unstable and that is all across the board.

Psychologists are mentally unsound people treating mentally unsound people with pills and that's an unsound way to treat the neurosis. Unless one applies this remedy to unveil right brain that person will never get better they will just be sedated enough from pills to just silence their mind all together.

Abraham and Lot were not butchers they were actually trying to save the species from itself.

[Genesis 19:13 For we will destroy this place, because the cry of them is waxen great before the face of the LORD; and the LORD hath sent us to destroy it.]

[because the cry of them is waxen great] = mental suffering

All these disorders are simply human beings mentally suffering because they have been conditioned into extreme left brain by traditional education. There is the odd brain tumor person who is exhibiting strange behavior but the vast majority are simply human beings of unsound mind exhibiting fruits of an unsound mind.

Agoraphobia - Intense anxiety about being in places or situations from which escape might be difficult or embarrassing. Simply a panic attack from emotions being turned way to high from being in X state of mind caused by traditional education. Embarrassment is simply a symptom of fear.

Pre-traditional education / pre eating off the tree of knowledge [Genesis 2:25 And they were both naked, the man and his wife, and were not ashamed.] = no shame or embarrassment

Post traditional education/ post eating off the tree of knowledge = [Genesis 3:10 And he said, I heard thy voice in the garden, and I was afraid, because I was naked; and I hid myself.]

So Agoraphobia = [and I hid myself] = Intense anxiety about being in places or situations from which escape might be difficult or embarrassing.
This is all relative to fear: embarrassment, shame, shyness, guilt.

Anorexia Nervosa – this is simply a child that has their mind bent to the left so they see parts, a left brain trait, and then they have embarrassment and shame about how they see their self so they starve so they will look better, but they never look better. The deeper reality is they simply have their ego and pride turned up so much as a result of the X state of mind they see their self as bad and that is simply a symptom of low self esteem. This low self esteem can be maintained for years and years because the thought processes are sequential and slow in X state of mind. One will never find a young child around the age of four or five that's has this disorder because education starts at six and one may never find a child that has this disorder until the absolute symptoms of all that left brain sequential education starts kicking in at about the age of ten and fourteen.

Asperger's Disorder - Hans Asperger, who in 1944 published a research paper which described a pattern of behaviors in several young boys who had normal intelligence and language development, but who also exhibited autistic-like behaviors and marked deficiencies in social and communication skills.
[normal intelligence and language development], these kids are just shy and embarrassed. The education bends the mind to the left example from 0 to 100 and ones who do well in education get their minds bent almost to 90 and some get it bent to 80 and some to 70 and all of these stages show different mental and emotional side effects. The point is the tradition education is bending the mind to the left so there are many, many conditions that occur from that bending. There is no test in civilization to determine how far the mind is bent because we are not talking about physiological aspects or being able to tell from looking at the brain, this bending is all on a mental level, an intangible as a result so the only way to tell is the fruits or behaviors of that being.
I'll make up a disorder – Mind senses time disorder, One is afraid of words disorder, One is afraid of shadows disorder. Now civilization can invent some more medicine to treat these people's disorders I suggest are simply hallucinations caused by an unsound, left bent mind. You are going to have to think very hard because I lost my fear of death by accident and my mind no longer senses time and I am no longer afraid of words, and I am no longer depressed, and I am not longer embarrassed, and I am no longer ashamed or scared of shadows or ghost yet I was very much so before I accidentally defeated my fear of death. So if your mind senses time you perhaps should not be in the psychology field. If you fear words you perhaps should not be in the psychology field prescribing drugs to people. How are you able to prescribe powerful mind altering drugs to people when you are in fact hallucinating? Perhaps the people who allow you to prescribe psychological drugs to people are also hallucinating like you are. You have no reason to fear as long as you didn't get any traditional education.

Attention-Deficit/Hyperactivity Disorder (Hyperkinetic Disorders) – What this really appears to be is a child who has their right brain unveiled a great degree which explains the fast talking, trouble organizing (a right brain trait), inability to follow rules(right brain trait), makes careless errors(careless is relative) which means they are unable to sequence things very well.

The darkness see's the light as darkness. The adults see the innocent children who have their right brain unveiled to a greater degree as bad or evil and so the adults who have their left brain bent all the way see a sound minded child as bad. The darkness seeks to kill the light because the light reveals to the darkness what the darkness is. All I see is insane lunatics trying to make a child who still has their right brain unveiled a good degree forcing the child to get their right brain veiled all the way. Why don't you stick some pills in the child and make some nice kicks backs and then the child will be more like you, and ruined like you. Get this in your pin prick mind. Right brain hates rules and hates to follow directions because it hinders right brains random access and pattern detection. Right brain is random access so it is not concerned about getting everything in a sequential order. Right brain is very powerful which explains why the child is hyper. For example I write 13 books of greater value in the same time you can write 1 book of lesser value. I am not hyper. I have right brain unveiled so I am simply not a mental sloth abomination any longer. I apologize I keep forgetting insane people know not what they do. Now that I ruined this book I will have to write another one.

Bereavement : That is what this comment means. [Matthew 8:22 But Jesus said unto him, Follow me; and let the dead bury their dead.] People have their emotions turned up so high because of the X state of mind instead of being able to accept the loss of a being their emotions make that event stick in their mind and every time they recall the memory it has lots of emotions tied to it. It is called coveting. They are so emotionally attached because their emotions are turned up so high in the X state of mind, when they lose someone they emotionally collapse. When a man's wife divorces him and he goes out and kills her, that's bereavement. When a man leaves a woman and she kills herself that is bereavement. That is all relative to the emotions being turned up so high because the mind is bent so far to the left as a result of the traditional education. Bereavement is a symptom a person who is mentally unsound is crying over split milk from a leaking container.

Bipolar : this is just a person who is feeling long periods of mood swings and the long periods of mood swings are only possible when the mind is bent to the left, X state of mind, so instead of having a moment of happiness and a moment or sadness and then ending up in neutral in sound mind this person simply has a prolonged swing. This is relative to the slothful nature the thoughts progress in the sequential left state of mind. A person with extreme depression or prolonged depression is the same thing as this except they do not have such pronounced manic episodes. They lean to just depression and this person has the depression and then they have the manic aspect but both of these situations are symptoms of prolonged emotions, and heightened emotions caused by being conditioned into the left brain extreme state.

Body Dysmorphic Disorder : This is the same thing as Anorexia Nervosa. A person in extreme left brain see's parts and so they see this one part of their body and they focus on it and they wish it was better or looked better. One of sound mind, with right brain unveiled is so cerebrally active and they see everything holistically so they do not notice parts or their body, like nose, chin, hair because the thoughts again are so fast one cannot maintain a state of lust to fix these parts of their body. It is lust. They lust to fix or alter a part. Their thoughts are sequential and slothful so they can focus on this part they do not like and it become all consuming. They are self haters of course all X state of mind beings are self haters. They hate who they are and that is expected from a being that is of unsound mind caused by their mind being bent to the left. The deeper reality is they are ashamed of their own body and they fear their own body because they are of unsound mind because they got traditional education which altered their perception and this altered perception makes them see their body as bad and they perceive they are bad so they are suffering because they are not bad they just had their perception altered so they perceive they are bad, they only see parts, a left brain trait.
The ambiguity and paradox combined with the fast pondering speed of the right brain keeps the person always in a state of questioning how they feel. A person cannot achieve a state of "knowing" they are depressed or sad and also a person cannot achieve a state of "knowing" they don't like their body or how they look. What this does is keeps a person emotionally neutral and emotionally stable. This is why the ambiguity trait of right brain is so valuable relative to ones emotional state. The ambiguity trait keeps the mind guessing how one feels about their self and about how they look. The processing speed when right brain is unveiled always keeps one on average emotionally neutral. One is in an emotional state of indifference and that means they have no anxiety or stress in contrast to how one is with their mind bent to the left, where that person knows their body is bad or their weight is bad or their appearance is bad and that is what causes the anxiety. The ambiguity and the processing speed of right brain is what keeps a person who has experienced a traumatic event from stressing out and from anxiety when they recall that memory because the time stamps and emotions are not translatable, is one way to look at it. A traumatic event is reduced in the mind to a picture without the emotional stamp and so one is indifferent to that picture and thus they do not get the stress and anxiety caused by that memory. It all comes down to one reality. The traditional education bends the mind of a child to the extreme left and then the game is over for them so a major shock to their mind is required to undo that extern left brain mindset state, which is what remedy does. Psychologist's minds have been bent to the left, and the patients minds have been bent to the left, and so the conclusion to just fill that patient with pills is also a fruit of a mind that has been bent to the left. Unsound minded people treating unsound minded people with unsound remedies. - 2:51:22 AM

12:01:16 PM - Bulimia Nervosa – This is a where a person eats and then binges. This has very little to do with a person having trouble with food. This is relative to a person who hates their self. A house divided cannot stand itself. A person who has plastic surgery is just like this person and this person is just like a Body Dysmorphic Disorder person and is just like this person Anorexia Nervosa. A drug addict or a person that cuts their self is just like these people. The core of all these disorders is simply the persons perception is altered as a result of the left brain bent education so they are in fact totally insane and they hallucinate and believe purging or binging or altering their looks with surgery will make them feel better but it never does make them feel better. A person in X state of mind will do things that harm them for money and this is the same thing. A person eats and then binges to feel better. A person in X state of mind will risk their life by doing things that they perceive will make them feel better but it never does make them better for long.

This comment [Genesis 2:17 But of the tree of the knowledge of good and evil, thou shalt not eat of it: for in the day that thou eatest thereof thou shalt surely die.] is saying, once you get all that left brain education called the tree of knowledge it bends your mind to the left and you start seeing parts instead of seeing holistically and seeing things as parts is going to kill you eventually. The remedy to this left bent state of mind is extreme fear conditioning and because these people who are bent to the left mentally have so much fear they may never be able to apply the remedy to the left bent state of mind so they will die in one way or another as a result of the state of mind they have been conditioned into as children by traditional equation. With bulimia the person perceives this strong hunger symptom of being in X state of mind is damaging them. They eat because they perceive great hunger mentally and so they are satisfying their great hunger and then they purge the food because they perceive its make them fat or unpleasing looking. Some people in the X state of mind will work out with weights in an effort to make their body look good. That person is simply working out with weights to death because they cannot stand how they look. Being overweight is not a symptom of a person who eats to much it is a symptom that their mind is bent to the left from education and their hunger is way too strong. Once the mind is bent to the left everything goes bad. All these people are doing from drug addicts, robbers, over eaters are simply beings trying to become satisfied as the result of an unsound mind and they never are satisfied so they are suffering and they trapped in an infinite loop of self destruction. In the unsound state of mind their anxiety is so strong they are reduced to self harmers. Even a person who works out with weights every day to have a buff body is not helping their self they are harming their self. A person who runs marathon is not helping their self they are harming their self. A person who runs a business is not helping their self they are harming their self because they eventually stress out and become nervous about how the business is going. They stress out about supply and demand and their profits and how much they should pay their workers. The people in X state of mind are never at peace they are always full of anxiety. They are stressed out about what has happen and what is happening and what will happen. Their mind is unsound and is against itself.

[Mark 3:25 And if a house be divided against itself, that house cannot stand.] A mind that has been bent to the left after years of sequential education is an unviable mind and creates an unviable being. There is no human who got this education and did not apply the remedy that is mentally viable. It is not possible they could be mentally viable so they are not a viable being unless they apply the remedy and unveil right brain and return to sound mind. There are no exceptions to that reality, there are just humans who are in infinite denial, and then the humans who are showing these obvious symptoms of self harm that are aware something in not right at least subconsciously or in their right brain, which is veiled.

The deeper reality is civilization encourages this traditional education on children and so it makes children mentally unsound, left bent mind, and so civilization itself is a self harmer of its own offspring. Civilization harms its offspring and then in turn is harmed because it has to watch its own offspring suffer and that bring suffering back to civilization.

There are physiological or disease related mental problems, actual diseases or genetic defects and everything else is the result of the mind being bent to the left as a child. A better way to look at it is one either has a brain tumor the size of Manhattan or they got the traditional education. The rule of thumb is if one actually senses time mentally they cannot be hallucinating or mentally unsound greater than that. If one can sit down for 15 minutes relative to a clock and then tell it's been 15 minutes they cannot be hallucinating more than that. If one has to eat every four hours because they get hungry and weak they cannot be hallucinating more than that. If a person is afraid to use a certain word around certain people for fear of being labeled uncivil they cannot be hallucinating more than that. If a person cannot understand years of sequential left brain education in fact does bend the mind dangerously to the left so one is left hallucinating, they cannot be hallucinating more than that. - 12:59:21 PM

1:09:32 PM – The Neurosis is so powerful the one thing a person can do to escape the neurosis, apply the remedy, is the one thing they perceive is most dangerous. You do not perceive anything is more dangerous than getting into a situation that makes your hypothalamus give you the signal you are going to die and then you do not run but you submit and do nothing when that signal is sent. You do not think anything in the universe is more dangerous than that, and that is your only salvation so you have to deny yourself, your thoughts, because they are all backwards. There is an old Turkish proverb that says something like, "Behind every brave man is a lion." You go seek the shadow of death and relative to you will perceive actual death, death from a shadow, as if you have no other purpose in the universe. As if you were born to seek the shadow of death so when you find it you will not run but ignore it. Until you get mentally to that state of mind you will never escape the mind trap you are in fully. You have to love death and seek death and that is the most unreasonable thing you have ever heard because you see truth as lies.

[Luke 17:33 ; and whosoever shall lose his life shall preserve it.] You would tell this being they are a liar and a fool and evil and hateful, and you would spit on them, and you would want them to be butchered for saying such comments. It is not that you wouldn't do it because you did do it, because you are a self harmer so you kill anything than can help you, and that achieves the self harm. There is an infinitely good chance your fate is already sealed, which means you cannot escape the place you have be thrown to mentally, so I just say what comes to mind to fulfill my contractual obligations. After all I am just a humble accident you were not ready for. - 1:19:46 PM

2:07:20 PM – When resurrecting the mentally dead, never reason with them. Because they are not aware they are dead, they will suggest it is best to be dead. Because they are not aware they are dead they will insult you for not being dead like they are. They will boast about all the benefits of being dead with the understanding they are boasting about all the benefits of being alive. One will have a tendency to attach to the dead because they feel sorry for the dead, so one has to at all times keep focused on suggesting the remedy to the dead, so the dead can wake up, but avoid acknowledging the questions of the dead. The one answer the dead do not want to hear is the way to be resurrected because then they have to face the fact they are dead. The dead are pleased with being dead because they are ignorant to the fact they are dead. One has to be indifferent to the dead because one tends to attach to the dead. The dead see the living as dead. The dead see the children as dead and so they want to make the children alive, which means they want the children to be dead also. The dead see the ways of the living as bad. There is a small area of cross over or what is known as overlap. It is what is known as the bridge between the living and the dead. The river Styx is a river of anger. Only through that river of anger can the dead come into life. This is why the 9th level of hell is treason. Treason against one's self is the river of Styx, the river of anger. So this treason level is the overlap between the living and the dead. The living cannot become angry and the dead perceive its best to avoid anger. So the dead perceive it is best to avoid treason against their self. The dead perceive it is bad to deny their self. The dead will always assist the dead around them to avoid the circle of treason. The dead want to keep everyone else dead and that way they will not have to face their self. Some of the dead will isolate their self away from the population of the dead and the population of the dead will attempt to bring that isolated dead back into the population. The population of the dead will create ideals that suggest when one of their dead isolates itself that is bad. The dead will suggest one of the dead that isolates their self is anti-social but in reality the population of the dead is saying "We do not want you to find life." If one of the dead isolates their self they may find a way out of hell but if they rely on the populace of the dead in hell that populace will always attempt to convince that isolated one it is best to remain in hell, so they will suggest it is best to remain with us. A lost sheep is a person who is dead and they wander from the herd, isolate, the populace of the dead, and they have a chance to get out of hell.

7:18:52 PM – I am getting back logged.

This is relative to Dante's explanation of hell. Hell is the state of mind one is conditioned into after the traditional education or as a result of the traditional education. The reverse world known as civilization wants to keep the people it conditions into this hell state of mind always seeking the first circle of hell which is limbo. In limbo one who is conditioned is the furthest they can be from waking up or from the 9th circle which is treason. Civilization knows not what it does so this is pushing people it has conditioned towards the first circle in hell is just a tendency of a group of insane people, or mentally unsound people. The ones who apply the remedy and get out of hell have a reverse goal. They want to drive the ones who are conditioned towards the 9th circle of hell which is treason relative to [let him deny himself]. So civilization wants to drive the ones it has conditioned further away from the exit of hell the 9th circle and the ones who apply the remedy want to drive the ones conditioned to the exit from hell the 9th circle, treason. That is what this means [Luke 17:33 ; and whosoever shall lose his life(treason ag"inst"the (self) caused by the education, left brain mindset to the extreme) shall preserve it(exit hell and preserve sound mind or unveil right brain, return to grace.)] So fallen from grace means ones gets the traditional education and their mind is bent to the left to a major degree and so they mentally fall from grace and then they apply the remedy and unveil right brain and return to grace.

This is the war of the opposites. Civilization wants to push everyone as far away from the exit to hell and the ones who escape hell want to push everyone to the 9th circle of hell. This is why when you make them angry you win because you are forcing them to cross the river Styx which is the river of anger. The ones conditioned see the river of Styx as fire and danger so they keep away from it but they have to swim across that river to escape hell and once in a while a ferry man will arrive, one who escapes hell, and they can make that crossing a bit easier for the ones in hell by explaining the reason they should cross that river they fear even though their mind is telling them not to cross that river. Because one has to go through hell, unsound mind, to get to heaven, sound mind, humiliation or detachment from material things assists one to get to that 9th circle. It does not have to be that way that is simply a trend or a pattern. All one has to do is seek a situation like a scary place at night all alone and get that hypothalamus to give them a "you are going to die from scary things" signal and then deny that signal which means don't run. One is going to have to use creativity to come up with a place that will scare them enough to make that hypothalamus give them that signal. Creativity is a right brain trait so that is going to be difficult so one has to go for broke. One wants to think of that one place on earth they do not want to be caught after dark alone out in the middle nowhere and that is exactly where they want to be caught. One can also scare their self to make the hypothalamus give that "death" signal. One can watch a scary movie, see a scary video, read a scary story and then simply turn out the lights go in the bathroom and look in the mirror and see if that works. There are many ways. There are many way to get that hypothalamus to give that death signal because it is not working properly, it is hyperactive. This is not suggesting you jump in a shark frenzy this is a mental

50

conditioning. You do not need a shark frenzy to scare you to death because you are scared to death of words, shadows, food, ideals and music.

This is the fast route [Luke 17:33 ; and whosoever shall lose his life shall preserve it.] Submit when the hypothalamus gives you that death signal is the fast route. Fear not when the hypothalamus gives you that death signal is the fast route. The reason you want the fast route is because it is also the full measure route. You want the chariot route so to speak because even when you do go the fast route you will experience a period of warming up and that is what this means [Mark 1:13 And he was there in the wilderness forty days, tempted of Satan; and was with the wild beasts; and the angels ministered unto him.] This comment is after John the Baptist applied his water remedy on Jesus. Your mind has been bent to the left since your were perhaps less than ten so right brain is not going to just unveil and then you're fine, you have to adjust mentally to having a shuttle rocket booster turned on in your head when you have been use to a moped engine as a mind since you were ten. The good news is right brain once the remedy is applied will do all the work you just go with the flow and expect all these things I suggest and right brain will [ministered unto him.]You will be just fine but you will have a period of adjustment to the new engine, mind set. The easiest way to look at it is after the education your mind is turn down to 10% cerebral power and once this remedy is applied you will need a period to adjust to 100% mind power. Once that happens you will have the opportunity to convince six billion lunatics they are lunatics and should apply the remedy you applied, and that is infinite job security because I am zero for six billion. The point is, experiment and see if you can come up with a practical way to accomplish causing the hypothalamus to give that death signal. When you unveil right brain, you call me and let me know what you think, when you are looking down at the sky. - 7:58:48 PM

12/8/2009 11:57:23 AM – I have already said too much to avoid the eventuality of what is going to happen because of what I suggest. You are not going to adjust your education methods and adapt the oral education because you are dead set on continuing the written education and so you are dead set on continuing to bend the children's minds to the left. You are not going to allow the child's mind to develop first by giving them oral education and then once their mind is developed you can teach them the written education. You are going to continue to put the children in a mental state of suffering like you put me in a mental state of suffering with your traditional education. I am not aware if I will be able to stop you but I am fully mindful I am going to give you a run for your money like you have never seen. This advice is for the ones who can see.

[Luke 20:46 Beware of the scribes, which desire to walk in long robes, and love greetings in the markets, and the highest seats in the synagogues, and the chief rooms at feasts;]

All I can suggest to a child is to tell your parents you want strictly oral education until your mind develops so your right brain is not veiled. You tell your parents if they force you to get traditional education you will sit in class, but will never write a word or attempt written math or memorize the abc's or memorize the number system. Chances are your parents will beat you or use fear tactics to force you to get the right brain veiling education they got, because misery love company, but even if they beat you to death, tis well, because once your right brain is veiled your are mentally dead anyway, so look at being beaten to death as simply cutting to the chase. If you get the traditional education you will be robbed of the one thing in this universe that is most important and that is a sound mind.

Beware of the ones who push the script, written education, the scribes. They have lots of material wealth and they are civilization and they are the movers and shakers in civilization, and they will suggest love and pleasing words to entice you to get their "brand" of education. They will sit in high seats of power and suggest mercy and compassion and God. They will have feasts to celebrate the fact they killed the truth. They will have feasts of material wealth to get you to get the written education but you will never end up with material wealth you will end up with an unsound mind and a slave job. Once you get the scribes "brand" of education you make a pact with the beast, and you will end up as the beast.

Are you starting to get the picture of why these wise beings in the ancient texts were butchered?

Peter was crucified head down in Rome, 66 A.D.

Andrew was bound to death. He preached until his death in 74 A.D.

James , son of Zebedee, was beheaded in Jerusalem by the sword. (Acts 12:1-9).

John was banished to the Isle of Patmos, 96 A.D. (Rev. 1- 9).

Phillip was crucified at Heirapole, Phryga, 52 A.D.

Bartholomew was beaten, crucified, then beheaded by the command of a king, 52 A.D.

Thomas was run through by a lance at Corehandal, East Indies, 52 A.D.

Matthew was slain by the sword in the city of Ethiopia about 60 A.D.

James son of Alphaeus, was thrown from a pinnacle, then beaten to death, 60 A.D.

Thaddeus was shot to death by arrows, 72 A.D.

Simon was crucified in Persia, 74 A.D.

This is what civilization, the cult, does to human beings who try to warn the common people of the dangers of traditional education.[Luke 20:46 Beware of the scribes] So you see this is why all bets are off. There are no morals and there are no rules when dealing with a cult that mentally rapes innocent children. That cult calls itself civilization and the sooner you understand that is absolute reality, the sooner you will understand one thing. Notice all these cities where the wise beings were killed are in different loca'ions. You+re looking at how vast the cult is. John was the one who was locked in cage so they silenced the light and thus they killed the light. John was not butchered but he was caged and silenced by the cult. The cult is as far and as wide as you can see. There is no point in anything, if at the end of the day, the cult gets to keep mentally raping children, is there grasshopper? There is no room to be compassionate and merciful when innocent children are being mentally raped is there grasshopper? We will consider morals after the battle grasshopper. All I am doing is talking to myself in my own personal poorly disguised thick pamphlet diaries so clearly I am no threat to any one, am I grass hopper? The reason these wise beings were killed or silenced is not because they were suggesting supernatural. That is not a threat to the cult, civilization. Supernatural is relative to the observer and because of that it is not a threat to civilization. These wise beings where saying this .[Luke 20:46 Beware of the scribes]. That is real. There are beings who make sure all the children become scribes and that means they make su'e the children+s minds are bent to the left, and that means the person is then mentally only capable of sequential thoughts and a bonus prize is their emotions and thus fear is turned to unstable levels and that is a perfect way to control a person. Leaving them with sequential thoughts and leaving them susceptible to fear tactics. That is a real threat to civilization because these wise beings were not only telling the common people of this brainwashing tool but they also had the remedy to the brainwashing. Not only were these wise beings telling people the traditional education was mentally hindering them, they were proving it by assisting ones to apply the remedy and waking people up. That is a threat to civilization, the cult because every single person that wakes up the full measure, will start waking up others by suggesting to them the remedy. The correct answer to every question I ask you is perhaps. - 12:26:45 PM

5:50:06 PM –The universe is a true vacuum. There is energy and there is matter. There are various types of exotic matter and exotic energy in this true vacuum. All of the energy and all of the matter make up Menergy. The gas tank in the true vacuum is at 10 gallons of Menergy and that never changes. The only thing that is real in the true vacuum are illusions of motion and illusions of change, energy transforming into matter and matter transforming into energy, but they are all none the less illusions because they do not alter the amount of Menergy. The only thing that is real in the true vacuum are thoughts and thoughts are relative to perceptions, so perception caused by thoughts are the only real thing in the true vacuum yet they are not tangible in a true vacuum. So one in the true vacuum who's perception is altered so they only see parts will see many parts and many motions and many things changing, but that is only relative to their perception. The ultimate reality is the 10 gallons of Menergy in the true vacuum never changes, and relative to that, nothing is all that is happening in the true vacuum.

"The secret to creativity is knowing how to hide your sources."-Albert Einstein
The secret to creativity is right brain so it is best not to veil it.

He was just a comedian in hiding. - 6:01:15 PM

6:24:11 PM –
Bartholomew was beaten, crucified, then beheaded by the command of a king, 52 A.D.

A king is the powers that be, left brain influenced containers in a position of power. Today a king would be the government. Bartholomew was running around telling the common people the traditional education, script, was putting them to sleep mentally and the king found out about it and the "king" silenced Bartholomew. Keep in mind a "king" had John the Baptist's head cut off. A "king" had Jesus crucified. A "king" had Socrates drink the hemlock. Keep in mind they use to feed the ones who applied the remedy to the lions.

Anyone who applies the remedy has the potential to wake up the entire world if they are not stopped. That is an indication of how fast the right brain operates. The quick and the dead, it's not in your head. The right brain gets better when it has a setback. The right brain gets better when the odds are impossibility. The right brain gets better when it has no chance to win. One simply cannot defeat something that gets better when it loses. Right brain wants to lose because it learns more from a loss than a win. How can one defeat something that wants to be defeated so it gets better? If one lets right brain win it will not stop and if one lets right brain lose it will get better and so the only option is to turn it off. Bartholomew was beaten, crucified, then beheaded by the command of a king, 52 A.D. This is why in these cases there is never a good reason for them killing these beings who applied the remedy. Right brain will change everything relative to the "kings" if it is allowed to continue. Right brain will free all the "kings" slaves if it left to its own devices, so to speak.

[Exodus 8:1 And the LORD spake unto Moses, Go unto Pharaoh, and say unto him, Thus saith the LORD, Let my people go, that they may serve me.]

And right brain which Moses had unveiled decided it was an impossible task to free the people from the taskmaster, so right brain decided to free the people so it could tell them how they could also free their minds, unveil right brain, for no other reason but, it was an impossible task.

Pharaoh = King = Taskmaster = the ones who push the traditional education.

This comment is speaking about the nature of right brain.

"Our greatest glory is not in never falling but in rising every time we fall."
–Confucius

If one learns from every failure then failure is winning, so then there is no failure or winning but only learning. This is why right brain is the perfect machine when unveiled. The ambiguity in right brain makes one question what a loss is and what a win is, so eventually these results are looked at as one thing, an event to come to further understandings. After one unveils right brain they will get the impression they are learning so fast that certainly it must end somewhere, and it never does end. This is relative to the concept no beginning and no end. An end is a failure or a win, but right brain does not acknowledge a win or a failure so there is no end and thus no beginning. I finish a book and right brain suggests I should clarify what I wrote in the last book by starting a new book, and that is about one minute relative to a clock after I finish the last book. I am expecting satisfaction to be achieved eventually but I cannot get no satisfaction and thus dissatisfaction, so I call it neutral. Perhaps it's best for the taskmaster to keep a machine like right brain veiled, perhaps. The tragedy is when right brain has been veiled these concepts are very alien and not really even possible because they are traits of right brain once it is unveiled.

Try Forever - http://www.youtube.com/watch?v=Tt47mpan-ms

 Once you understand the comment below is simply saying traditional education is a form of brainwashing used to push the mind to the sequential based, slothful aspect of the brain one will understand traditional education in fact makes one unwise or stupid and not wise at all.
"If you reflect back upon our own educational training, we have been traditionally taught to master the 3 R's: reading, writing and arithmetic -- the domain and strength of the left brain."
Once you understand that is all that is happening in education then one can start pondering the remedy to negate this left brain bent state of mind. - 6:53:28 PM

"Great spirits have always encountered violent opposition from mediocre minds."
-Albert Einstein
This comment convinces me Einstein did not know the tree of knowledge veils the right brain. I am not suggesting any human being on this planet has a mediocre mind relative to an absolute. I am suggesting there are six billion Einstein's that had their right brain veiled by traditional education and that is also not an absolute because thanks to the wise beings in the ancient texts they discovered the remedy to unveil right brain after traditional education has veiled it.
So I will clarify Einstein's comment by saying: Sound minded beings have always encountered violent opposition from potentially sound minded beings.
And that leads to this comment : Being recognized by an important being is a treasure beyond value. - 7:25:52 PM

9:57:25 PM – I did some experimenting in chat rooms today and in summary: kicked in teeth, zero for six billion. I understand that is the result so I have gained a valuable understanding. The neurosis caused by all that left brain conditioning is so deep a person is perhaps permanently gone mentally or unable to ever escape that left brain extreme state unless they have an accident and defeat their fear of death. That's logical because to think one can negate years and years of left brain education in one fail swoop, so to speak, is not very realistic. The traditional education is very subtle so it is like taking LSD when a person is six and the LSD slowly starts working and is all full strength at about the age of ten or twelve maybe 14. So the person cannot even tell they are hallucinating because the "drug" kicks in so slowly. I certainly had no idea. I am an accident or a mistake or I defeated my fear of death accidentally and this shocked the hypothalamus into sending normal signals of fear instead of sending greatly magnified signals of fear.

These are some patterns and they are just patterns.

Buddha's words were found and memorized and so Buddhism is an oral tradition.

Jesus spoke orally.

Mohamed's words were transcribed by his friends so he suggested the Quran orally.

Native American sat around the camp fire and told stories of their history orally so their history was maintained by oral tradition.

Hinduism dates back 50,000 years.

Aboriginal religion dates back 60,000 years.

So the last two mentioned show religion existed and so did communication just not written communication at least not as we know it today.

Then we have these comments.

[Luke 22:2 And the chief priests and scribes sought how they might kill him; for they feared the people.]

[scribes sought how they might kill him; for they feared]

[Luke 11:44 Woe unto you, scribes and Pharisees, hypocrites!...]

A Pharisees in Hebrew means someone set apart, left brain see's parts. A scribe is a Sadducee; someone who favors written language over oral communication or relative to the exact explanation one who favor written law to oral law.

One who is a scribe is one who learns the sequential based education and their mind is bent to the left so they are mentally unbalanced or set apart mentally.

So, [scribes sought how they might kill him; for they feared] = [2 Timothy 1:7 For God hath not given us the spirit of fear; but of power, and of love, and of a sound mind.]

[For God hath not given us the spirit of fear;] = [scribes sought how they might kill him; for they feared] = [spirit of fear} caused by being a scribe, traditional education = unsound mind = mind bent to the left = mind set apart

So a scribe is a Sadducee and also a Pharisees = hypocrites. The scribes celebrate with feasts they call holidays to celebrate the fact they defeated the ones who suggested oral education. Christmas, Hanukkah, Easter, Lent, Passover and the list goes on forever. They are feasts the scribes/ Sadducee's use to celebrate they killed the wise beings or defeated the wise beings who suggested there was a problem with the written education, language/ tree of knowledge. One knows the scribes defeated the wise beings because written education, traditional education is essentially all there is now.

[Matthew 7:29 For he taught them as one having authority, and not as the scribes.] = He taught them orally and not using written, scribe educational methods. The written, traditional education veils the right brain and the oral education does not. The written education makes one mentally hindered or retarded and the oral education does not. If you want your children to be a retard give them the written traditional education and if you c're about your child+s mind give them the oral education. Those are your only two choices in this universe. But before you can make that choice you have to apply the remedy because you got the traditional education so you cannot make proper decisions because you are of unsound mind which is a nice way to say you are a lunatic.

Here is what you say about everything I say relative to these ancient texts. [Matthew 9:3 And, behold, certain of the scribes(ones who got the w'itten education and didn+t apply the remedy, left brain influenced) said within themselves, This man(one who was under the influence of right brain) blasphemeth.]

Be mindful once one applies the remedy they can use the language but they will not be very good at it relative to spelling or arranging the letters in proper sequence without some effort. One may not be able to apply the fear not remedy, the full measure of waking up but one can meditate and say the word perhaps a lot and start to slowly unveiled right brain some. Only the ones who are close to the 9th circle of hell, treason, perhaps will be able to apply the remedy the full measure relative to [Matthew 5:3 Blessed are the poor in spirit (ones close to or in the 9th circle of hell, treason): for theirs is the kingdom of heaven.] The good news is in civilization there are many who are poor in spirit, drug addicts, prostitutes, criminals, ones with emotional problems, the poor and the list goes on. There a"e not"as many (kings) in civilization in contrast.

I was pondering who in civilization would be great candidates for this remedy and I understand people who consider their self Goths would be great candidates. They like cemeteries and haunted houses already, they are interested in death and so they perhaps would be interested in defeating their fear of perceived death. Relative to civilization "those who lose their life will preserve it" is suggesting death but in reality civilization, the scribes are mentally dead so the comment is really suggesting life and since one's mind will no longer register time after the remedy it is suggesting eternal life or the fountain of youth. So I am mindful I do not write these books for the wealthy and the well educated and the intellectuals because they will just spit at the spirit of what I suggest. I write for the ones on the fringe of civilization. For the ones who are not so indoctrinated into the ways of civilization, the cult. I write for the ones who say "I got twelve years of traditional education and it certainly didn't make me wise. If I am so wise how come I cannot think clearly and I have a slave job?" I do not pander to ones in civilization that try to blame people that are not mentally well, they are not trying hard enough. They are not applying their self so they can move up the ladder of civilization. All I hear from that talk is they want everyone to get up to that first circle of hell so they have no chance of escaping hell.

I understand the comment about Adam being the first man and Eve being the first woman is relative to, they were the first man and woman who "woke up" and wrote about the ill's of the tree of knowledge relative to that area of the world. - 12/9/2009 12:29:10 AM

3:56:51 AM – It is late and I am sloppy. I have been considering what the ones in the religious chat rooms I speak with have arguments about what I suggest. First off all across the board they do not get what the tree of knowledge is. Most do not see the name tree of knowledge as being important but the principle that God said do not eat off of it and man did eat off of it , so they see that as the main point relative to the tree of knowledge but do not consider the tree of knowledge as being of any importance. It could have just as well been a cup of wine and God said do not drink off of that and we did so we fell from grace. Because they miss the point of what exactly the tree of knowledge is relative to actual reality they do not grasp when they suggest the devil they ate off the tree of knowledge so they are of the devil. One might suggest that understanding does not go over well in the religious chat rooms. They will suggest they pray so the devil cannot harm them but they do not grasp if they ate of the tree of knowledge and have not applied the remedy they are praying to the devil. This devil concept is relative to the mental symptoms one exhibits after their mind is bent to the left and these symptoms are known as sins relative to the ancient texts and this hell concept is the state of mind one is in after the mind is bent to the left so that alone negates this supernatural devil/hell combination. I know what hell is, and I was in it for forty years. One can shoot off their mouth about what they know about afterlife and hell, but perhaps they should first try to get out of hell before they do that.

[Psalms 116:3 The sorrows of death compassed me, and the pains of hell gat hold upon me: I found trouble and sorrow.]

[sorrows of death] and [I found trouble and sorrow.] relative to [Genesis 3:17 . in sorrow shalt thou eat of it all the days of thy life;]

When the mind is bent to the left one is in sorrow because they need both aspect of the mind right and left to function properly and when do not have both aspects of the mind in 50/50 harmony all they can do is suffer. We are born with the right brain unveiled and at the age of six we start favoring left brain with the sequential education and this in turn veils the right brain mental aspects. Perhaps one should keep their supernatural opinions to their self just in case they are hallucinating out of their mind. This comment almost proves it beyond a shadow of a doubt that this tree of knowledge alters the mind and makes one mentally suffer.

[Deuteronomy 28:65 And among these nations shalt thou find no ease, neither shall the sole of thy foot have rest: but the LORD shall give thee there a trembling heart, and failing of eyes, and sorrow of mind:]

[sorrow of mind] [sorrows of death] [I found trouble and sorrow.] [Genesis 3:17 . in sorrow shalt thou eat of it all the days of thy life;]

This is a good one. [Ecclesiastes 1:18 For in much wisdom is much grief: and he that increaseth knowledge increaseth sorrow.]

[and he that increaseth knowledge increaseth sorrow.] = [Genesis 3:17 And unto Adam he said, Because thou hast hearkened unto the voice of thy wife, and hast eaten of the tree, of which I commanded thee, saying, Thou shalt not eat of it: cursed is the ground for thy sake; [in sorrow shalt thou eat of it all the days of thy life;]

With wisdom, unveiling right brain come grief because once one wakes up they fully understand what this traditional education has done to our species mentally and it has done so much damage one has moments of grief or frustration. Moses called it anger waxing. The absolute depths of the grief is that we have six billion genius minds that are bent to the left, and thus 10% minds when they can easily be 100% minds with just a moment of mental self control. It seems like it can be

58

fixed in one second and it's no big deal to fix it, but it is perhaps never going to be fixed.

[and he that increaseth knowledge increaseth sorrow.] this comment is relative to the more traditional education one gets the more sequential conditioning one gets and the more the mind bends to the left and thus the more sorrow one has mentally. If child gets one year of traditional education and let's say they only memorize the abc's and do not learn how to spell or read then their mind will not be bent to the left as far as a person who get 5 years of traditional education and learns how to spell and read and learns math and that is what this means [and he that increaseth knowledge increaseth sorrow.] If one wants to get into speaking about the devil they better call their parents the devil, everyone they know the devil, their fellow countrymen the devil, the governments the devil and most of all their self the devil, because they all push traditional education. Convincing you to get out of hell is not paramount on my list. Convincing you to stop putting children in hell, like you were put in hell, is paramount on my list, boy. - 4:43:30 AM

1:49:56 PM – I spoke with someone in a chat room and told them the situation with traditional education and they said "Without education we would all just be sitting around doing nothing." I saw great wisdom in that comment because I see wisdom in the words of fools. I became aware that person was right on the money and not aware he was right on the money, so to speak. I am not a contributor to civilization because I unveiled the machine, right brain and I am just a thinker now, and thinking is intangible so I am sitting around doing nothing, relative to civilization that perceives doing something is a physical task. Building a house, hauling wood, flipping burgers, running a store are all doing something but thinking is not doing something it is doing nothing, intangible, so I am not a contributor to civilization, I am just a loser who is lazy and does not do anything, or does not contribute to civilization. If I go outside and dig a hole to the center of the earth, at least I am doing something more than just thinking, which is nothing. "Don't think just do something tangible so you can charge for it."

"Go chop down that forest so people will buy the wood so they can build a house no one will ever live in and then you will be a valuable contributor to civilization." When you lose the machine, right brain, you lose your ability to think and then you are stuck with a slave job that accomplishes stupidity.

Is there any reason we are still building houses? Are we short on houses or are we just building houses so the people who build houses will have a job and can say they contribute to civilization. If one is just doing and not thinking then what they are doing is not thoughtful.

Civilization has these unspoken norms that are subtle manipulation mechanisms. Beings indoctrinated into civilization have these three words they always throw around as if they were true. The three words are "You have to.." You have to be a productive member of society. You have to make money to live. You have to conform to civilization to exist. You have to get an education to survive. You are going to get civilizations "brand " of education or you are going to get the shit beat out of you by the minions of civilization, is a better way to look at it. I see too many genius minds that get just enough education to ruin their mind and then they get stuck with a slave job, and then they are told their genes are bad or their mind is not good enough to get a good job. I do not have any choice but to write in my personal diary I spit in the face of civilization and everyone who believes in civilization, the cult. I do not want to hear some brainwashed, sequential based, pin prick, ruined mind suggesting to me that is not proper to say. I do not want to hear some pin prick, sequential based, brainwashed mind questioning the validity of what I write in my personal diaries because if they had a sound mind they would be fully aware they are not allowed to question one single sentence I write in personal diaries. If they could think they would understand it is best not to question what I write in my diaries. I had to go through too much hell to unveil right brain after civilization veiled it, to give a shit about what any human being on this planet thinks about what I write in my personal diaries. Simply put, relative to my perception you do not even fucking exist. I cannot be biased against something that does not even exist. You go back to your little slave job and I will sit here and think, which is what you call doing nothing. I tell you what reality is and you go insane trying to figure out how it can't be true. That's our little pact. I torment you in the mental hell you have been put in by civilization, and maybe if I torment you enough you will get to the 9th circle, treason, and have a good accident and get out. That is as good as it is ever going to get for you. So if you stop reading my personal diaries you are doomed to never leave mental hell, and if you keep reading my personal diaries you are doomed to be pushed further down the circles in hell. I cannot show anyone my picture but I look like a people. Shhhhhh. Zero for six billion has a nice texture to it.- 2:25:51 PM

4:13:24 PM - The main psychological or mental remedy to unveiling right brain is relative to this comment [Mark 8:34 And when he had called the people unto him with his disciples also, he said unto them, Whosoever will come after me, let him deny himself, and take up his cross, and follow me.]
[let him deny himself]. So saying 'perhaps' often is in fact denying yourself, and yourself after traditional education is the left brain bent personality. The next conditioning to prepare yourself to unveil right brain is another form of humiliation or prostration. This form of humiliation is helping one deny what they do like and accept what they do not like.
Liking something or disliking something that is inanimate is abnormal. A judge is a person who determines what is good and what is bad. The deeper reality is a person with their mind bent to the left, because 'f traditional education, see+s parts because parts are a left brain trait. That is relative to this comment [Genesis 2:9 And out of the ground made the LORD God to grow every tree that is pleasant to the sight, and good for food; the tree of life also in the midst of the garden, and the tree of knowledge of good and evil.]
[good and evil.] = seeing things as parts and contrary to that right brain is holistic so right brain does not see things as good or evil but see's everything as one

thing. So, one who unveils right brain tends to see everything as good. This is relative to a child who trusts everyone. A child will trust anyone including people who want to bend that child's mind to the left. This is also relative to the fact the Native Americans trusted the "white man" and the "white man" took everything they had and put them concentration camps. So one can argue seeing everything as one thing or seeing everything as good is bad thing, but that is only relative to the fact civilization are simply a group of unsound minded lunatics because they were forced to get traditional education by a group of unsound minded lunatics. In absolute reality seeing everything as good or holistically is very mentally healthy. So one has to condition their mind to stop seeing parts and that requires what is known as self control so they can fulfill [let him deny himself].

Music is a fantastic tool to accomplish this with. All this exercise is doing is freeing up your right brain a bit until you get to a point you can apply the main remedy. One is aware of what kind of music they like so one is aware of what kind of music they dislike. That like or dislike is abnormal because sound is just sound. There is no genre of music in reality it is all music and all music is sound whether there are vocals or just drums it is still just sound. So the genres of music in civilization is a symptom civilization has their mind bent to the left and it see's parts. Some in order to correct this abnormally one has to pick out music they hate or dislike the most and listen to it until they start to become indifferent to it and this requires self control. What I mean is I am fully aware you dislike some kinds of sounds because your mind is bent to the left and that dislike of some sounds has nothing to do with you having a taste in certain music, it has to do with you showing symptoms of an unsound mind.

Here is some of my music .

Buy Me - http://www.youtube.com/watch?v=jvhLoY0OY1A

Some say - http://www.youtube.com/watch?v=LYSFpuLPsX0

If you like this music do not listen to it and find music you dislike. If you hate it, listen to it until you are indifferent. This is the reverse thing again and that is relative to [let him deny himself]. You do not want to go to a scary dark alone and defeat your fear of perceived death, the shadow of death, and that 's why you have to in order to escape the mental hell you are in. I am attempting to show you the way to escape the hell you were put in by civilization but I am mindful many do not want to escape hell because they do not believe they are in mental hell. Not everyone is supposed to escape hell, only the lower tier in the circle of hell are suppose to escape hell generally speaking, the poor in spirit. My words are a sifter. The material goes into the sifter and the sifter sifts out the chaff and all that remains is the wheat. The chaff fall back to hell and the wheat remains above hell. What that means is I write as I am compelled to with the understanding the seeker will not be intimidated by the words and the chaff will flee in terror by from the words. So no matter what I say the wheat will not run away from the words and the chaff will come up with infinite reasons to run away from the words. That is how it works. That is how it has always worked. I may write harsh and bitter and angry words and perhaps a depressed angry bitter person will read them and feel better about their self because they will understand they perhaps are not as bitter and angry as the one who wrote these books appears. I am mindful I can only relate to the ones in the lower tier of the circle of hell and I perhaps cannot relate to the one in the higher tier. So the wealthy and the rich relative to civilization that have no applied the remedy are pretty much write offs before I even type a single word. They will see one comma out of place and flee in terror and come to sequential conclusions they perceive are accurate. They will see one misspelled word in these books and they will have a nervous breakdown. So I understand these books are a tool unto their self because they separate the nervous wrecks from the beings who can take anything and are ready to "wake up". When I was depressed and I saw a book titled "Love, love love", I thought get that book out of my face. A depressed person does not want anyone to tell them about love. A depressed person is trying with all their might to escape the mental hell civilization has put them in, with its wisdom education, and then all civilization wants to do is tell them about the word love and compassion and mercy and justice. Civilization will use its little words to entice one top stay in mental hell but the depressed are immune to those feel god words because they are subconsciously aware of reality. Civilization is bending innocent children's minds to the left on an industrial scale and if civilization submits it does in knowingly it will be slaughtered and if civilization submits it does it unknowingly then it certain cannot possible know what love is, because its love is hate, its compassion is destruction, its mercy is torture and its justice is injustice. Before you go spouting off how much love you have, please be mindful you knowingly or unknowing support the mental rape of sound minded innocent children. Who say you I am?

Rest your head old friend. It's the end old friend.
Old friend - http://www.youtube.com/watch?v=shCnh5lIT8Y - 5:04:25 PM

1:59:35 AM –
I oft wish; return the sea;
Resume its slumber; forget me.
Some never do know just how
Tis cold and dark thy golden bough

12/10/2009 4:40:03 AM – It's harder to be easy going than going easy. The most complete way to fail is to perceive you can. Ambiguity is the best safeguard from defeat. Doubting you won also means doubting you lost. Achieving a goal is not as important as seeking goals to achieve. A seeker never finds and a finder oft quits. Finding an understanding is not as good as seeking a better understanding.
10:21:20 AM – The concept of nirvana or nothingness or neutral is suggested because the right brain when unveiled has ambiguity and paradox. A person after unveiling right brain may eat some food and then try to determine if it tastes good or tastes bad and their mind will say, it may taste good and it may taste bad, and that's the ambiguity aspect and then the paradox aspect says its takes good and it tastes bad, and these are the minds final answer. When a person tries to think how much time has pass the mind says maybe lots of time and maybe no time, the

ambiguity aspect, and then says no time has passed and lots of time has passed, the paradox aspect, and that is the minds final answer. This ambiguity, paradox aspect applies to the sensation of pain. Applies to when a person looks at another person and also applies to when a person hears sounds or music. This concept relative to the ancient texts is simply one is unable to judge god or evil so to speak. When one cannot judge something as being good or evil they tend to be pleased with it.

[Genesis 3:16 Unto the woman he said, I will greatly multiply thy sorrow and thy conception; in sorrow thou shalt bring forth children; and thy desire shall be to thy husband, and he shall rule over thee.]

[Unto the woman he said, I will greatly multiply thy sorrow and thy conception] Female is the serpent and is a contrast statement for describing a human who eats off the tree of knowledge and does not apply the remedy. Greatly multiply sorrow is relative to this judgment aspect that happens when right brain is veiled. One"goes around saying (I know this is good and"I know that is bad.) One feels a little pain and they suffer because the ambiguity and paradox is no questioning how bad the pain is, the mind knows how bad the pain is. Because the being ate of the tree "f kno"ledge their minds (knows) how bad the pain is. Because they ate off the tree of knowledge the being knows what foods tastes good and what foods taste bad, what music sounds good and what music sound bad, and of course what is right and what is wrong, what is good and what is evil [Genesis 2:9   the tree of life also in the midst of the garden, and the tree of knowledge of good and evil.]

The tree of life is oral education and the tree of knowledge of good and evil is written education. The education one gets is the exact same education except with the tree of knowledge education the mind gets bent to the left and one starts knowing good and evil because they start seeing parts because seeing parts is a left brain trait and because they veil right brain as a result of all that sequential written education they veil the ambiguity and par"dox. "hen one sees parts and (knows) what is good or evil they start to desire what they perceive is good and desire to avoid what they perceive is evil. [and thy desire shall be to thy husband, and he shall rule over thee.] So the husband of that person is the extreme left brain state and it is their perception that they become a slave to, and false perception. I am not suggesting 'ales are false, although there won't be many females insulted if I do. One+s mind bent to the left determines what they like and so they desire it and they do many things to get this thing they desire but once they get it is never satisfies them.[and he shall rule over thee.]. They are slaves to desire, and what they desire is not really what they desire it is simply what their mind in is left bent state tells them they desire. This leads to greed, gluttony, lust and envy. One should not need something materialistically to be satisfied and when one does not get something they desire they should not be dissatisfied. One should not be going up and down the stairs emotionally as Dante suggested because it is a fo'm of suffering that is the result of one who+s mind is bent to the left as a result of all those years of traditional education. Of course in an economic system the powers that be and the economic system itself relies on one always desiring one more trinket so they feel satisfied. Until the mind breaks free of this left brain bent perception one will always desire and the desire will never end. Some in civilization will suggest that desire motivates one so it is proper. Killing someone over a grain of sand, a little oil, a pair of shoes, some drugs is not proper. Charging your fellow man usury rates because you desire to make some money is not proper. Paying workers as little money as possible because the owner desires to make a healthy profit is not proper. When people are worth less than all then the material things one desires then people are less than worthless. This planet has the potential to grow enough food for everyone ten times over except someone desires to control the amount of food so they can make it scarce because they desire to make a profit and on top of that everyone minds are bent to the left so they are hungry, desire for food, all the time because when they think "f they are hungry the"r mind says (I"know you are hungry) instead'of saying (May'e yo" are hungry or maybe you aren+t hungry.) And that+s the final answer from the mind. One does not feel hungry three times a day, desire, to the point they get weak when they do not three times a day their mind is just bent to the left and [and thy desire shall be to thy husband, and he shall rule over thee.]. No one will ever say it better than Adam said it [Genesis 2:17 But of the tree of the knowledge of good and evil, thou shalt not eat of it: for in the day that thou eatest thereof thou shalt surely die.]

[thou shalt surely die.] = [greatly multiply thy sorrow]

Once the delicate is bent to the left one cannot be doing anything but suffering and one cannot be in any state of mind but a suffering state of mind. The tragedy is a person as a child trusted people who also had their minds bent to the left and now that person has to go through some major fear conditioning to get out of that left bent state of mind and that is also suffering, because their fear is through the roof and the remedy is fear not.

The only reason you do not go to a crowded room with your peers and yell out a profanity, and a profanity is simply a word you perceive is a bad word because your mind knows good from evil in its left brain, seeing everything as parts extreme state, is because you are scared to death to say such an evil word. [[Genesis 2:17 But of the tree of the knowledge of good and evil] You ate off the tree of knowl'dge and you see everything as either good or evil and if it+s not like you it is evil. Since the Native Americans are not like you they certainly must be evil relative to a person with an infinitely unsound mind. If a person skin color is not like yours they certainly must be evil relative to a person with an unsound mind. If a person religion is not like yours they certainly must be evil relative to a person with an unsound mind. If a person does not believe what you believe they certainly must evil relative to a person with an unsound mind. I do not see anyone as evil because I fully understand they have been conditioned into an unsound state of mind juts like I was conditioned into an unsound state mind except I accidentally applied this ancient so one can regain their sound mind after they get the tree of knowledge. It serves no purpose to punish someone in extreme mental sorrow because they are in an unsound state of mind. A person of sound mind cannot be fooled very often and a person of unsound mind can be fooled consistently. Perhaps one should consider that very carefully in relation to why the powe"s that be, go out of the"r way to make sure (no child is left behind), as far as the traditional education goes. I attempt to reach you but because you see anything different than yourself as evil, you only see me as evil. If I think you are evil, I certainly have a funny way of showing it. - 5:31:50 PM

7:18:06 PM – So this war that has been going on for over 5000 years is a symptom of one thing.
There is the Sadducees who push the written education because they got the written education as a child and so their mind is bent to the left so they are not even aware at all when they pus' that same education on innocent children they bend the children+s mind to the left and leav' that child in a mental state of suffering for the rest of that child+s life. Then there is one' who push the oral education or the education that does not bent the child+s mind to the left. They are aware of the perils of the tree of knowledge and so they are mindful and cautious when administering it. There is nothing else going on here in this reality you called the human species but a war between these two factions, these two adversaries. The ones with their minds bent to the left perceive the ones who suggest oral education for the children are wrong or bad or insane or stupid. That reality is the core of the battle. There is a planet full of mentally unsound insane people who are factually harming innocent children mentally and they do not even know they are. There is a comment relative to some religions that suggest never try to reason with the devil and that comment alone is why there is war. One simply does not reason with an insane person who is factually mentally harming children on a level that is beyond cruelty and does not even understand they are mentally harming children on a level beyond cruelty. So there is nothing else happening in this location called earth relative to mankind except mentally sound being who are the minority trying to stop mentally unsound being who are the vast majority from mentally destroying the children which is the life spring of the species. So we are really not doing anything as a species but trying to keep our head above the frozen lake. We are frozen as a species because all we are doing is trying to protec: our self from our self. I would be pleased to end this piece of crap poorly disguised thick pamphlet nightmare diary on that note, but there is no end. There is no peace. There is no time to rest. There are being right now on this planet who are attacking the schools of the ones who push the written education and in turn are mentally harming innocent children and these beings are being slaughtered wholesale, because they are fighting a physical battle against six billion insane people and these being do not complain because they understand one comment from these texts few will ever understand. [John 15:13 Greater love hath no man than this, that a man lay down his life for his friends.] These being lay down their lives in droves fighting against six billon humans they are trying to protect the children from the sane and the sane think they are wise to kill them. The sane are thinking how stupid these beings must be to lay down their life and be slaughtered by the sane wholesale. These beings are attempting to continue a 5000 years old tradition of human being trying to stop mentally conditioned unsound human

65

beings from further destroying the life spring of the species, the minds of innocent children. The sane will suggest these being are attacking our schools with our innocent children because the sane do not understand they"are o"ly raping the children mentally with their (brand) of education. I however am infinitely blessed because the sane cannot understand a single word I say. So the next time you run your mouth and suggest the words peace, love, happiness or freedom, you be mindful you only suggest those words because you are infinitely ignorant to the reality all around you. There is no freedom of choice when society itself pushes the traditional education on you when you are an innocent six year old child and this education bends your mind to the left and totally alters your perception so everything you do in life after that education is relative to the fact someone made 'ou how you ac" by altering you" perceptio", using fear tactics like"(If you don+t get our (brand) of education you will suffer.) So never ever say the word freedom because I am already bogged down writing infinite books trying to explain how ignorant you are, and I certainly do not need you to clarify it anymore than you already have. You are free as long as your definition of freedom is a brainwashed, sequential based, pin prick mental joke, unknowing mental rapist of innocent children, caged abomination. As long as that is your definition of freedom then you should go to the highest mountain and scream out , let freedom ring, because it certainly is ringing in my ears. Thousands of years ago they were telling people this [Genesis 45:19 Now thou art commanded, this do ye; take you wagons out of the land of Egypt for your little ones, and for your wives, and bring your father, and come.] They were saying get away from civilization"becau"e civilization is going to one way or another force their (brand) of education on your children and one your wives and then you will wake up one and wonder why your children are addicted to drugs and why your children hate you, and hate their self, and wh' your wife hates herself and hates you and hates the children. For your own children+s sake and sanity [take you wagons out of the land of Egypt(civilization that pushes the written education) for"your "ittle ones]. You do not do it for yourself because you got the (brand) of education, you do it for the little ones because they still have a chance. You consider yourself expendable because I assure you that you are expendable and the earth is my witness. What that means is y"u are"w3illing to die to make sure your children do not get civilizations (brand) of education, traditional education, and if you are not willing to do that, then you do anything you want to do no matter what it is, because you have no conscious at all. If you are willing to allow innocent children with perfectly sound complex minds to be mentally hindered into a state of mental sorrow you have the green light to do anything you want because nothing in the universe is more sinister than doing that to an innocent children. Once you mentally rape innocent children you do whatever you want because you will never be forgiven for that.
[Mark 9:42 And whosoever shall offend one of these little ones that believe in me, it is better for him that a millstone were hanged about his neck, and he were cast into the sea.]
One I better off typing a stone around their neck and throwing their self into the sea than to stand by and allow an innocent child to have its mind bent to the left

so that child is left in a mental state of suffering. One is better off running into a wall of lead and bombs than to stand by an allow civilization to bend the minds of innocent children so the children are left in a mental state of suffering. One is better off dead because the children are the life spring of the species and when they are conditioned into an unsound state of mind the species in turn is dead. You are dead if you allow that to happen to children because we are dead if you allow that to happen to children and that child is dead if you allow that to happen to them.

M. P. (14) committed suicide by hanging from the clothes rod in his closet

L. W. (14) allegedly took her own life

S. M. (14) allegedly committed suicide by hanging

S. O. (14) allegedly committed suicide by hanging

K. A. (14) allegedly took her own life for unknown reasons

K. O.(14) took her own life by an unknown method

V. S. (14) allegedly took her own life

B. B. (14) committed suicide by hanging

A. S. (14) was found hanging in her closet

On one hand, one might suggest these innocent children did not take to well to having their mind bent to the left by traditional education. On one hand one might suggest having their mind bent to the left to the degree their emotions were turned up to maximum did not work out to well for them. On one hand you are looking at actual proof the comment give me liberty or give me death is playing out every day. On one hand these children are telling their parents and civilization, "Since you mentally raped me I will take a rope and hang myself with it to show you what your fruits are." For these children it was better for them to tie a rope around their neck and cast their self into the sea. [it is better for him that a millstone were hanged about his neck, and he were cast into the sea.] It was better for them to kill their self than to go on with life in the mental state of suffering their parents and civilization unknowingly put them in. Civilizations handy work is quite impressive. Fourteen is right about the time the years of left brain sequential traditional education drives the being totally insane. One can simply think back to when they were fourteen and remember they had some sort of emotional problems from drug abuse to run of the mill emotional problems and now they will understand why. Some have it worse than others but that makes it a mystery, because when bending innocent children's minds to the left one never knows what might happen. Sometimes the emotions being turned up to the extreme do not catch up to the person until later.

C. J. (19) killed herself after battling with depression

P. L. (18) hanged himself after a battle with depression

C. H. (17) committed suicide by hanging himself because of depression

B. S. (18) allegedly committed suicide by overdose after a battle with depression

K. B. (19) took his life after suffering from depression

It is simply hard to tell how long the children will last after they get their mind bent to the left and have their emotions turned up to maximum as a result. No matter how one wishes to t'ink about it they will never be able to explain any better than it was explained thousand+s of years ago [Mark 3:25 And if a house be divided against itself, that house cannot stand.] A mind bent to the left means the being is no longer viable without a major shock to their mind to get it to go back to sound mind. Whether it means a person will eat their self to death, drink their self to death, stave 'heir self to death, stress their self to death, die trying to make money, die because they can+t make enough money the bottom line is one is essentially a ticking time bomb on a suicide mission. - 8:54:34 PM

10:33:51 PM - I just saw a commercial where they were selling a 50 cent collector coin for $19.95 and at the end of the commercial the announcer said "Order now to avoid disappointment and future regret." and I fell out of my chair. - 10:36:12 PM

12/11/2009 12:09:16 AM – The deeper reality to this remedy is one has to deny their self after they get the traditional education. One has to go through the 9th circle of hell, treason, to escape hell. One has to lose their life to preserve it. The children above opted to leave hell and they took the only route out of hell, treason, deny their self, those who lose their life will preserve it. Once in a while a person commits this treason and escapes hell but they are tapped to hang around a bit longer before they move on. Once one eats off this tree of knowledge their mind is bent to the left and they are in mental hell and hell is suffering and no matter what they do there is only one way out of the suffering of hell and that one thing is the one thing a person in hell does not want to do. The angel you fear holds the key out of here.

[Exodus 23:20 Behold, I send an Angel before thee, to keep thee in the way, and to bring thee into the place which I have prepared.] .- 12:16:37 AM

3:57:35 AM – "All that we are is the result of what we have thought"- Buddha

All that we are not is the result of what we have not thought.

One cannot control what another person thinks unless they alter that person's mental perception.

I cannot make you fear my words but if I alter your perception so you are susceptible to fear I can make you fear my words. I cannot make you afraid of shadows but I can later your mental perception so you will be susceptible to being afraid of shadows. If I can convince you there is evil and then convince you if you think or say certain things it is veil then I control your thoughts and your actions and your words.

[Genesis 2:17 But of the tree of the knowledge of good and evil, thou shalt not eat of it: for in the day that thou eatest thereof thou shalt surely die.]

[But of the tree of the knowledge of good and evil] = minds perception is altered so one perceives good and evil, parts, a left brain trait.

Where is this evil you are certain there is? Perhaps I am evil for saying there is no evil. If I agree with everything you think you will assume I am good and if I disagree with everything you think you will assume I am evil. Evil is relative to the observer. If you think any word spoken is evil you are absolutely right but only relative to you, not relative to absolute reality. Civilization is not evil just because it forces the traditional education on innocent children and leaves those children in a mental state of suffering for the rest of their life. That is not evil it simply just is. Traditional education relative to absolute reality bends the mind so far to the left the person is mental unstable and thus mentally hindered to an extreme. That is not evil it just is. There are no animals on this planet that are capable of evil but apparently people are capable of evil. People that are mentally unstable as a result of being conditioned to be mentally unstable as children are not evil. This comment [Genesis 2:17 But of the tree of the knowledge of good and evil, thou shalt not eat of it: for in the day that thou eatest thereof thou shalt surely die.] This comment is saying no one is evil, but the ones who get all the left brain conditioning will perceive evil. Once a person starts to perceive evil they are what is known as paranoid and they are dangerous to their self and those around them. These texts mention wicked and that is a nice way to say mentally unstable or exhibiting mental traits of one who is unstable but it is not saying evil.

There is no evil unless you perceive there is and if you perceive there is evil, it is because you got the traditional education and your mind is seeing everything as parts. [Genesis 2:17 But of the tree of the knowledge of good and evil, thou shalt not eat of it:] This is saying there is no evil but if you get traditional education your mind will be bent to the left and you will start to perceive good and evil, parts, a left brain trait, so thou shall not eat of that tree. If one wants to become paranoid and delusional eat of that tree and if one does not want to become paranoid and delusional do not eat of that tree, traditional education. It is an If then statement.

If ' gets traditional education" then delusional and perceives good and evil, parts, a left brain trait.

If "does not get traditional education" then one is of sound mind and does not perceive good and evil but see's everything as one thing or holistically, a right brain trait.

The pecking order relative to the brain and thus the mind is when left and right brain are equal in dominance 50/50, then one tends to exhibit right brain and left brain traits but right brain tends to dominate in some aspects. I see many things as one thing but I can sequence. I can see parts but I doubt them. I see people who I perceive do bad things but I doubt they are bad things. I am fully aware right brain is excellent at complexity and paradox and I am fully aware my texts are full of contradictions which are symptoms of paradox, and that is an indication of the flaws in written language not the flaws in right brain or in my thought processes. Society looks at someone who says contradictions as someone bad, evil or insane, so society looks at right brain as bad, evil or insane. Psychologists look at someone who says many contradictions as sick, or mentally unstable so psychologists fill them with pills because psychology dislikes right brain. Neither society or psychologists are evil for doing that, but none the less they do that.

A rhyme is a symptom of right brain detecting patterns in the sounds. Boy, toy, Roy, coy. Those are patterns and right brain is a master at patterns. That is a good trait of right brain and very few would ever detect a person who says rhymes in songs or poems as being mentally unsound or mentally ill. But then there is the paradox and thus contradictions and many consider those things a symptom of a confused mind. Intuition is considered a good aspect by many and that is simply street smarts contrary to left brains intellect which is book smarts. In many situations in life street smarts are far more valuable than book smarts because intuition has no boundaries and intellect does.

The Native Americans made great scouts not because of their intellect but because they had great intuition because their right brain was not veiled because they did not have traditional education.

Creativity is a right brain trait and creativity is relative to intuition. One cannot go read in a book how to be creative they can just get ideas by looking at others creativity. A human being with creativity and intuition veiled is suffering because they should have those things at full power. Nature meant us to have those mental aspects at full power or nature would have veiled them when we were born. One needs all the right brain traits at full power in order to comb out wisdom from knowledge, comb out wisdom from reading a book.

I am pleased to talk about Orwell's book 1984. The thought police are coming in 1984 is certainly what I thought when I read that book before the accident. I was taking everything literal and on face value and that is what intellect is. Intuition has nothing to do with face value and combined with the ambiguity of right brain ones tends not to take anything on face value relative to knowledge and that is what thinking out of the box is. Intuition is relative to seeing things that are not said in a sentence or story.

This comment [Genesis 2:17 But of the tree of the knowledge of good and evil] does not say many years of sequential based left brain education will makes one perceives things as parts because a left brain trait is seeing things as parts. I am 100% factually certain that is what that line says but because you have been conditioned into extreme left brain and have not applied the remedy you are intellectually reading that and taking it on face value and I am getting the spirit of that comment using intuition. I am not suggesting I am wise or special I am suggesting right brain is better left unveiled. If you want to veil something veil left brain. Right brain has all the heightened awareness aspects so if you veil that you are simply left being unaware of all things going on around you. Eventually everyone comes to a problem in their life and the answer is not in a book and so they need the full power of intuition to solve that problem or they will panic and determine the problem is unsolvable or too great a problem and that situation is not a good road to be on.

C. W. (38) shot himself and his wife in a murder suicide after he lost his job .

When people have their right brain veiled and thus have their intuition, ambiguity, complexity, and creativity turned way down, a simple problem can appear to be the end of the road for them. The deeper reality is one in this left brain extreme state of mind panics in the face of a problem, their sense of time is turned way up and so they are impatient, and one who has right brain unveiled doubts there are any problems. That is very funny because in one Hindu room I went into early after the accident I spoke to someone and I told them my situation and the man replied "No problems." A better way to look at it is you lay every problem you can think of on right brains shoulders and it will thank you for giving it something to ponder and solve. Right brain see's everything as one thing and that one thing is an opportunity for it to ponder and think on.

One of the first things I said to my infinite wrath potential after the accident was "I want to live."

There is this cerebral sensation when right brain is unveiled and everything in the universe makes perfect sense and this makes a being want to live just because everything is all of the sudden simple.

You want to solve world hunger? Start applying the remedy and assisting the ones who have had their minds veiled so they won't sense such strong hunger and they will all stop eating so much. Simple.

You want to solve all the stress and anxiety and emotional problems, Assist people with applying this remedy so they unveil their right brain. Simple.

You want to solve the drug problem. Assist ones with apply this remedy so they will not need to do drugs to escape the mental suffering caused by being in the extreme left brain state of mind caused by traditional education. Simple.

You want to stop all the wars and hate in the world, assist people with unveiling their right brain with this remedy. Simple.

You want a world of Einstein's? Assist people with this remedy and attempt not to veil children's right brain by using oral education until their minds fully mature. Simple.

With the right brain veiled everything is impossible and with the right brain unveiled anything is possible, and it is that simple. If only you believed.

"Education is hanging around until you've caught on." - Robert Frost

Apparently everyone is a comedian.

Education made me wise to the fact education doesn't make one wise. The truth is only a threat to liars. What you see is perception, what you know is inflection. It's better to believe nothing than everything. That last comment doesn't look right, but I doubt it. - 5:25:11 AM

12/12/2009 4:03:22 AM - "Those who cannot remember the past are condemned to repeat it." - George Santayana

"Only the dead have seen the end of war." - George Santayana

George was a philosopher from Spain. Those who cannot remember the past are doomed. There are two versions of the past relative to mankind. One version is true and one version is false. If one believes the false version they will continue to repeat the past. If one believes the true version they have a chance to escape repeating the past and thus leaving that infinite cycle.

The first version of the past relative to mankind is. Mankind invented written language and math and mankind greatly improved his wisdom and these two inventions greatly improved mankind without question.

The second version is mankind invented written language and math and this caused mankind to mentally drown because it altered mankind's mind as a result of learning these inventions and mankind went into a deep mental suffering called hell.

So the comment "Only the dead have seen the end of war." Is the exact same thing's as saying "Ignorance is bliss". The ones who believe the first version of the past are mentally hindered and are the mentally dead so they are totally unaware of the war and so for them there is no war. The ones who understand the second version is the true past are mindful the war is anything but over. Mankind is trapped in an infinite loop because it believes the first version of the past. The ancient texts suggest the second version of the past. All we can do as a species is attempt to come to the understanding written language and math are tools that have a devastating effect on the mind of a child if not taught properly by masters who understand those devastating mental side effects.

[Genesis 19:13 For we will destroy this place, because the cry of them is waxen great before the face of the LORD; and the LORD hath sent us to destroy it.]
[Genesis 19:24 Then the LORD rained upon Sodom and upon Gomorrah brimstone and fire from the LORD out of heaven;]
[Genesis 19:25 And he overthrew those cities, and all the plain, and all the inhabitants of the cities, and that which grew upon the ground.]
[and the LORD hath sent us to destroy it.]
[Then the LORD rained upon Sodom and upon Gomorrah brimstone and fire]
[and all the inhabitants of the cities]
Us = Abraham and Lot
Lord = right brain
And the right brain did its calculations and determined it was best if Abraham and Lot destroyed the cities and all the inhabitants, left brain influenced containers, of the cities because right brain understood with its intuition there was no way they could convince the men of the cities of the perils of written language and math on the mind because men of the cities already got the education and were mentally hindered, and Abraham and Lot had to try and stop the spread of this mental drowning the traditional education caused.
A cancer cell is simply a mutated cell and one of its traits is uncontrollable growth, division beyond normal limits. One might suggest cancer cells overpopulate. A cancer cell does not see itself as abnormal. Only an observer of the cancer cell understands the cancer cell is dividing beyond normal limits. Another cancer cell does not see a cancer cell as abnormal so the division beyond normal limits appears to be normal relative to a cancer cell. So one might suggest a cancer cell knows not what it does because eventually that cancer cell will kill its host and in turn kill itself because of its division beyond normal limits. In the same manner one who gets traditional education does not perceive they reproduce beyond normal limits. One who gets the traditional education and does not apply the remedy does not see anything abnormal about their behavior. Only someone who applies the remedy or never gets traditional education can see behavior of ones who get the education and do not apply the remedy as abnormal. A better way to look at it is one who get the traditional education and then applies the remedy understands their behavior before the remedy was abnormal. The cancer cell is going to kill the host eventually and also kill all the healthy cells along with it, if

left unchecked. And that is all this means [[Genesis 19:13 For we will destroy this place, because the cry of them is waxen great before the face of the LORD; and the LORD hath sent us to destroy it.]

We will destroy the cancer because the cancer is a threat to the host, the species. So what Abraham and Lot did was righteous. A doctor has a patient with cancer and that doctor tells that patient they have to have chemotherapy to kill the cancer. That chemotherapy's main goal is to nearly kill the patient in hopes that nearly killing the patient will literally kill all the cancer cells. The doctor is righteous for doing that although the doctor is literally harming the patient. This is relative to the remedy to the tree of knowledge. The patient, ones who gets the education, has to face the shadow of death and relative to them it is death, in hopes facing death will kill off the cancer, the unsound mind, and return them to a sound mind, or cure them. No patient wants to get chemotherapy but equally no patient wants to die. No person who got the traditional education wants to face death but equally no person that got traditional education wants to remain mentally unsound. No person wants to be mentally unsound and in a position they have to defeat their fear of death to return to sound mind, but civilization does not give anyone that choice. - 5:09:49 AM

11:31:13 AM –

"We can't know the consequences of suppressing a child's spontaneity. Perhaps we suffocate life itself. We must respect this first individuality." - Maria Montessori 1912

Spontaneity is impulse behavior. Creativity is impulse behavior. Intuition is impulse thoughts. Contrary to spontaneity is planning. One goes to school to hear the teacher's lesson plan. One goes to school to see how many rules they can cram in their head. If one follows the rules they are good and if they do not they are bad. Another way to look at it is the more rules one follows the less they rely on intuition, creativity and thus spontaneity.

" We don't need no education.

We don't need no thought control

No dark sarcasm in the classroom

Teachers leave them kids alone." - Pink Floyd   THE WALL   1979

Once a person gets even a few years of the traditional education, their mind starts bending to the left and then their thoughts become sequential based and they start to become shy and embarrassed and thus nervous and very emotional and so their thoughts are controlled. [Hey teacher leave those kids alone.] Teacher are you sure you are not just being used as a slave making tool?

B. P. (14) committed suicide for unknown reasons. – I understand what the unknown reason is. I am not suggesting from time to time a child gets all that sequential education and is mentally hindered I am suggesting every single child that goes through the traditional education system is mentally ruined for life unless they apply the harsh fear not remedy for countering all that left brain education. You prepare yourself mindfully for the battle and forget about compensation because rapists do not compensate their victims except with more rape.

"A general state education is a mere contrivance for molding people to be exactly alike. It establishes a despotism over the mind, leading by natural tendency to one over the body." Harriet and John Stuart Mill   1865

Despotism is tyranny, dictatorship, absolutism. Words represent absolutism. For example if a child misspells a word they are scolded for being stupid or dumb because there is only one way to spell a word right relative to traditional education and that is absolutism.

"I swear upon the altar of God, eternal hostility to every form of tyranny over the mind of man." – Thomas Jefferson. If one believes Jefferson would stand by and allow this traditional education, left brain favoring education, to happen to children unquestioningly, one is simply ignorant. Downfall is only relative to those who perceive they are on pedestals. Happiness is relative to ignorance and wisdom is relative to grief. Happiness is relative to intellect and intuition is relative to grief. A blind man can walk on a battlefield of corpses and praise the smell of the roses.

"Textbooks shall "romote citizenship, emphasize patriotism and respect for recognized authority. (Textbook content shall not encourage life-styles deviating from generally accepted standards of society." - Texas State Board of Education 1982

[Textbook content shall not encourage life-styles deviating from generally accepted standards] relative to ["We don't need no thought control. Hey teacher leave those kids alone."] I am not concerned what a tyrant thinks about freedom. Perhaps right brain does not perhaps take kindly perhaps to being veiled perhaps. Perhaps you perhaps will understand perhaps exactly perhaps what that means perhaps infinitely sooner perhaps than you can perhaps ever imagine perhaps, perhaps. Perhaps Neurotics perhaps cannot perhaps tolerate ambiguity perhaps, perhaps. Perhaps a person has no conscience or morals or class if they would stoop perhaps to such a low perhaps that they would invade the private diaries of another person perhaps without that person's permission, perhaps. - 1:22:36 PM

6:02:34 PM — [Matthew 16:6 Then Jesus said unto them, Take heed and beware of the leaven of the Pharisees and of the Sadducees.]

Leaven = expansion

Pharisees = prefer oral education

Sadducees = prefer written education

Jesus was attacking everyone, left brain containers. That is what is known as being self righteous but in reality he was really trying to help them understand the situation caused by written language but they were mentally hindered so they simply are mindfully unable to fully get it, so to speak. This is trait of one who unveils right brain because one loses their ego, they are under the influence of right brain and right brain has no room for ego and extreme concentration. This state of neutral when one unveils right brain means one is always trying to break out of neutral. A being in the left brain conditioned state of mind tries to maintain one state of mind. They are either depressed or happy and these states of mind are prolonged. For example a person can appear happy all their life and then one day they lose their job and go ballistic and society says "He was a good man and we are surprised because he had no criminal record and he appeared "normal." In the state of neutral one can appear manic because they are in neutral and so they show symptoms of depression and manic behavior but they always end up back in neutral. The deeper reality is that words are absolutes and there are perhaps no absolutes relative to words. A better way to look at it is right brain has paradox, complexity, ambiguity and intuition and words fall short of being able to explain those things. When ones intuition and random access has already figured out they cannot win in convincing civilization that traditional education in fact devastates the mind of a child, they over compensate. I am already fully aware I will not be able to convince the powers that be relative to civilization that traditional education is devastating to the mind of children that has not even developed fully. Since I am already fully aware of the end conclusion, what I do to reach that end conclusion does not change that end conclusion. This is relative to the Catholic comment about possession: Do not reason with a demon. I cannot convince you of anything and you cannot convince me of anything relative to the only thing that is important. I am suggesting to you traditional education destroys the mind and you are suggesting to me it does not. You are suggesting to me twelve years of left brain education does not bend the mind to the left and I am suggesting it does. I cannot convince you and you cannot convince me. I can write infinite books that you cannot argue with the spirit of, and you will still conclude it does not mean traditional education bends the mind to the left. At the end of the day you will not apply the remedy because you do not believe the traditional education you got bends the min to the left. At the end of the day you will put a bumper sticker on your car and boast to the world how well your child is doing so in traditional education. At the end of the day you will still tell me a child hangs their self at 14 for unknown reasons. Any way you want to look at it, I am going to continue to cram my books down your throat until you stop breathing.

A small deed is a great deed in planning. The fear of limits and the limits of fear are better experimented with than believed. Compassion for ignorance is ignorant.- 6:41:51 PM

12/13/2009 2:11:56 AM — [Galatians 4:10 Ye observe days, and months, and times, and years.]
I am quite certain the ones in the Amazon who never had traditional education do not have watches. They perhaps do not even have calendars. They perhaps do not even have birthday parties. One in civilization might suggest they are certainly uncivilized if they do not have watches, calendar's and birthday parties. A calendar relative to an economy lets the ones who charge usury interest rates know when they have made money for doing nothing. Usury is relative to calendar. The ones in the Amazon do not subscribe to usury. The ones in the Amazon do not see any reason to take advantage of their friends with this concept usury but they do not have the traditional education so clearly they are not civilized. Everyone knows

only the civilized take advantage of their friends and their own species with usury methods.

[Exodus 22:25 If thou lend money to any of my people that is poor by thee, thou shalt not be to him as an usurer, neither shalt thou lay upon him usury.]

These beings must be uncivilized also because they suggest one should not take advantage of their own species with usury. [thou shalt not be to him as an usurer, neither shalt thou lay upon him usury.] All this means is when you start charging members of your own species usury rates you make them your slave.

Now there is no carpetbagger that is going to buy this argument because they make a living off of making people their slave. There is no doubt in the universe about that.

[Deuteronomy 23:19 Thou shalt not lend upon usury to thy brother; usury of money, usury of victuals, usury of any thing that is lent upon usury:]

[Thou shalt not lend upon usury to thy brother]. Anyone in your species is your brother. When one takes advantage of someone in their own species they harm their self because they harm their own species. This is relative to what this left brain bent mindset, it has turned our species into self harmers. As a species conditioned into the unsound state of mind we harm our self.

[usury of money, usury of victuals, usury of any thing that is lent upon usury:] this is saying do not lend money or food or anything to your brother and charge interest because once you do you harm yourself because you are your brother and your brother is you because you are both a part of the human species. Before you know it everyone is charging usury rates and they cannot afford the rates so they lose their house and do not enough to survive on because they are paying all their slave money to the usury rates. I am not suggesting people in America charge usury rates because that would mean they are harming their own fellow citizens and that would means they are breaking a very important concept of America which is to form a more perfect union. I am quite certain there is no one in America that charges usury because that only encourages a more perfect separation.

[Deuteronomy 23:20 Unto a stranger thou mayest lend upon usury; but unto thy brother thou shalt not lend upon usury: that the LORD thy God may bless thee in all that thou settest thine hand to in the land whither thou goest to possess it.]

[Unto a stranger thou mayest lend upon usury; but unto thy brother thou shalt not lend upon usury:] What this means is one can charge usury on every other species on the planet but their own species because anyone in their own species is their brother. So it is okay to go charge usury rates on fish and snakes and snails and lions and sheep but you do not charge usury rates on your brother because when you do, you harm yourself because your brother is of your own species. We are all brothers because we are all human beings and if you can argue your way out of that one, you are infinitely wiser than I will ever be.

Granted it is important to be mindful of reality. There are no carpetbaggers that see anything wrong with usury. Who are the carpet baggers?

[Nehemiah 5:7 Then I consulted with myself, and I rebuked the nobles, and the rulers, and said unto them, Ye exact usury, every one of his brother. And I set a great assembly against them.]

[the nobles, and the rulers,] = The powers that be relative to civilization, the cult. [And I set a great assembly against them.] Do you see how these texts are against civilization, left brain influenced containers, and the nobles and the rules, and ruler denotes the taskmaster. The reality is these ancient texts are methods to defeat the taskmasters and the rulers who trying to herd everyone into confined space so they can be controlled. To clarify right brain influence is trying to bring left brain back into mental harmony but left brain wants nothing to do with that because in a 50/50 contest right brain always wins or is the dominate influence on the mind. The rulers veil the right brain of everyone as children and that makes that child narrow minded and susceptible to fear tactics and so they are easy to control and manipulate. What this means is even the taskmasters and rulers in civilization are mentally unsound, because they continue to publish these ancient texts, which are essentially suggesting methods their slaves can use to wake up, counter the brainwashing, and also methods to use to defeat the rulers and taskmasters, left brain, bring left brain back into the fold.

[And I set a great assembly against them.] who did he set a great assembly against? [the nobles, and the rulers,] Why the nobles and the rules? Because they were the ones pushing the traditional education on everyone, to make them mentally hindered and thus easy to control, making them slaves.

If you get enough of the "rulers" "brand" of education you will be wise, and then you can charge your brother usury rates and brag to everyone how civilized you are.

[Luke 19:23 Wherefore then gavest not thou my money into the bank, that at my coming I might have required mine own with usury?]

This is simply saying, if you put your money in the bank and you get interest the bank does not pay you that interest, some other guy, your brother, pays usury rates to the bank and the bank pays you out of those usury rates, so you are harming your brother. Do you see how these texts are anti-civilization? The correct answer to every question I ask you is perhaps. These beings were not killed because they said they believed in god but because they were a threat to the cult, civilization, the ways of left brain. Civilization is just like organized crime and if you get in their way they will find your body floating in a river or hanging on a cross or they will vote to make you drink hemlock or poison you with mushrooms or lamb chops. One is wise to understand what they are waking up to, before they wake up. - 3:00:18 AM

5:15:43 PM – Are you here to assist other people or are you here to assist yourself in hopes that will assist other people?

Those who forget the past repeat the past and that is relative to those who win the war get to determine the history of the war and that is relative to , to the victor go the spoils, and that is relative to might makes right.

The only way human beings can feel a sense of accomplishment is through cerebral understandings. So human beings because they were so intelligent put their self to sleep mentally with traditional education for the sole purpose or

77

understanding how to wake their self up again to feel a sense of accomplishment. So once in a while one of the human beings wakes up and attempts to wake up the others for no other reason but to come to further understandings. There is nothing else to do but to come to further understandings in infinity so the ones who wake up are not really trying to wake up other people as much as trying to simply improve their self and their own understandings. If one of these being s wakes everyone up eventually the species will put itself back to sleep for no other reason but to have an opportunity to come to further understandings. There is no other creature in the universe that has ever posed a threat to the human species so there is nothing to fight against but ourselves. Fighting against ourselves helps us come to further understandings and not fighting against ourselves helps us to come to further understandings. Some human beings understood a long time ago there is no threat to human beings in this universe because human beings are the most intelligent beings in the universe. These beings spoke of a supreme being and they were talking about human beings. These beings were trying to explain to the collective of human beings that we got lost in our own infinite intelligence. A being of our intelligence is going to get lost in its own intelligence just so it can come to understandings to escape that trap it had fallen into. It is not a question of if we are the most intelligent being in the universe the question is what are we going to do once we consciously understand that reality. Some humans understand that reality and they realized they could build up walls and weapons and posture for war with their self or they could relax and enjoy the ride. These being realized they could turn flat ground into a mountain to climb to reach flat ground or they could just settle for flat ground and make peace with the reality there is nothing else in the universe that can compete with human beings. The collective of the human species is waiting for something to show up and fight us because all we gave to fight is ourselves. We as a species are looking for a fight but there are no creatures who would dare fight us because they understand we get better when we lose. As a species we are like a bored child that is imagining this huge battle and imagining there is no way to win but at the last moment the child pulls out his secret weapons and wins the impossible battle. We have at times made other species look like they pose a challenge to us but in time we defeat them all. We at times try to make sharks look like a threat top us or bears or elephants or lions or diseases. We are simply trying to make a mountain out of flat ground because flat ground means we are the supreme beings in the universe and that means we have to relax and clam down and stop all this vanity. We are a being that is so intelligent we have to keep ourselves mentally hindered so there is perceived challenge, because in reality there is no challenge in the universe. To this day human beings have never been able to defeat their self because we are still here. Human beings do not create standing armies to fight against whales or sharks. We are simply trying to find one more understanding because we cannot learn because there is nothing to learn because we are perhaps the supreme being spoken of in the ancient texts and that is a prospect that is beyond our own understanding. We have nothing left to defeat in the universe but ourselves and we cannot ever do that. We are undefeatable unto ourselves so we are getting caught up in our infinite wisdom.

We make ourselves stupid so we can become wise and then we become wise and wish we were stupid and all that is really happening is we are coming t' further understandings. We destroy the environment so we can come to the understanding we shouldn+t destroy the environment and once we achieve that we destroy the environment again. All there is to do in infinity is try to make it seem like you are doing something. We try to get ourselves emotional and excited for this perceived battle but there is no battle it is just us in infinity and we are a bored child letting his imagine run wild to pass the time and there is only infinite time. We come to understandings and forget those understandings and find those understandings again and the illusion of progression is achieved. My purpose is to arrange words in order to excite emotions in order to come to the understanding I can arrange words in order to excite emotions. I have to talk to myself because I would insult you by trying to teach you, because you understand everything already. We understand therefore we are understanding.[Psalms 147:5 Great is our Lord, and of great power: his understanding is infinite.] Human beings are observers. Everything they hear, taste, smell, feel and see is directed to the cerebral cortex and translated into an understanding. If one goes outside they understand if it is night or day, hot or cold. On top of that they understand if it is very dark or very bright, or slightly dark or slightly bright, very cold or slightly cold, very hot or slightly hot. There are infinite variations of cold and infinite variations of hot because everything is relative to the observer. One person may perceive it is very cold and one may perceive it is slightly cold but no two people will ever sense the exact degree of cold even if they are all in the exact same temperature. Some people can jump into a ice lake and hardly be fazed and some people jump in that same ice lake and nearly have a cardiac arrest. The ice lake is the same temperature but the cerebral cortex is different in everyone relative to how it perceives the incoming signals. This of course is relative to perception. How many understandings does a person come to in an average day? They wake up and understand they were asleep. They take a shower and understand the water was warm. They brush their teeth and understand they need more tooth paste. They breathe in and understand they are breathing. They get something to eat because they understand they are hungry. They rush out of the house because they understand they are going to be late. The answer to how many understandings a person comes to in their life time is, more than they can count, and the definition of more than one can count is infinite.[his understanding is infinite.] Since every human being is simply coming to understandings there really is no good or evil understandings because an understanding is the result of the cerebral cortex trying to define a sensory perception. Sometimes a person will jump into cold water and just give out a grunt or a verbal sound to try to exp'ain this sensory perception that comes to their mind to explain how cold the water is.'Some just yell it+s very cold and some yell other words and then some just gasp for air to let others know it+s very cold. So the words cannot really explain all the cerebral sensations the cerebral cortex gives one. Since words cannot explain the infinite cerebral sensations the cerebral cortex can give a person relative to all the senses so one tends to settle for a word to explain the sensation but that word in not actually explaining the actual cerebral sensation. One in the extreme left brain state of mind tends to define all these cerebral sensations into two categories, good or bad, good or evil. That dinner was good or that dinner was bad. That person is good or that person is bad. That song is good or that song is bad. That word is good or that word is bad. This is a symptom of perceiving everything parts and that is a left brain trait. Notice some of these initial comments in genesis. God is seeing everything as one thing and that one thing is good.

[Genesis 1:18 And to rule over the day and over the night, and to divide the light from the darkness: and God saw that it was good.]

[God saw that it was good.] = God saw everything a one thing or perceived everything was good or perceived holistically which is a right brain trait.

[Genesis 1:25 And God made the beast of the earth after his kind, and cattle after their kind, and every thing that creepeth upon the earth after his kind: and God saw that it was good.]

[and every thing that creepeth upon the earth after his kind: and God saw that it was good.] = No good or evil (parts, a left brain trait), just everything was good, holistic, everything as one thing. So if everything is good then there cannot be any labels or parts. Nudity, that's good. Cuss words, that's good. Music, that's good. Drugs, that's good. Birds, that's good. Water, that's good. So all of these thing's are all good, so one can only describe them as, they just are. If everything is good then there is no contrast, so nothing is better than anything else so everything just is.

But then this comment comes up.

[Genesis 2:17 But of the tree of the knowledge of good and evil, thou shalt not eat of it: for in the day that thou eatest thereof thou shalt surely die.]

[But of the tree of the knowledge of good and evil] Now everything is not good, things have labels, good and evil, and those are parts and those require judgment and that is a left brain trait. With right brains ambiguity one is always questioning if things are good or bad and that tends to be the final answer. Maybe good or maybe bad and that is the ambiguity or right brain so when right brain is veiled after the tree of knowledge then one only see's things as good or bad. A better way to look at it is the sensory perceptions go into the cerebral cortex and the right brain is veiled so the cerebral cortex judges things as parts, good or evil because the ambiguity in right brain is silenced.

[for in the day that thou eatest thereof thou shalt surely die.] What is going to die if one east this tree of knowledge and it bends their mind to the left so they starts seeing everything as parts? This is what dies [saw that it was good.]. One's ability to see everything holistically. So this turns a world that one normally perceived as all good, into a world of monsters where ones sees things that are good as evil. So a child see's everything as good and trusts everyone and then they get the education and all the sudden they start seeing things they use to see as good, as evil. Their perception has changed but the objects they perceived as good as a child have not changed. As a child they did not see nudity as evil but now they do see nudity as evil. As a child they did not see what they see after the "education" because their perception has been altered. So one starts off as a child seeing everything as good then they get traditional education and start seeing those exact same things they use to see as good as evil so they have started hallucinating. They have become knowledgeable and that means they have started hallucinating because they see things they use to see as good, as evil. A child does not see any words as evil but after the education and some encouragement they start seeing words as evil. Are words evil? Impossible. A sound cannot be evil, but after one's mind is bent to the left and they start perceiving only good and evil, parts, they will start hallucinating and believing factually words can be evil. If one perceives nudity is evil then they are saying being born nude is abnormal and evil. Then they start seeing their own body as evil. Then they are doomed because they can never escape all the monsters of evil they perceive everywhere. Once a person gets enough traditional education they start seeing evil and they will spend their whole life trying to fight these evil monsters they use to see as good angels before the education. A person will cut their face so they will not see it as evil but before the education they saw their face as good so they are attacking their self because they are hallucinating because they are in an unsound state of mind caused by the education. A person may starve their self so their body will not look so evil but in reality their body is perfect it is just they are hallucinating and seeing devils when there are only angels. They know not what they do. I am blessed because no one can understand anything I say ever, into infinity. - 10:44:23 PM

12/14/2009 1:38:23 AM – One that can imagine they are important does not need to be important. Human beings used right brain creativity to invent written language and math and in learning written language and math that veiled right brain and silenced creativity. This is a good example of getting lost in our own extreme mind power. To intelligent for our own good would be one way to look at it. Beyond our own understanding would be another way to look at it.
Human beings used right brain creativity to invent written language and in learning that invention we veiled right brain and silenced creativity.

3:53:01 PM — [2 Timothy 2:13 If we believe not, yet he abideth faithful: he cannot deny himself.]
One can have all the faith in the universe but if they do not believe the many years of sequential traditional education has veiled their right brain they will never apply the remedy and the remedy is to deny one's self, to lose their self mentally to unveil right brain, to face the shadow of death and fear not, to knock the hypothalamus back into working order. One cannot tell their right brain is veiled because it was done starting at the age of six and was complete by the age of twelve or fourteen. I accidentally applied the remedy so I could not tell my right was veiled either so I know for a fact you cannot tell your right brain was veiled. So you are going to have to take my word for it and I have no credentials relative to the world you perceive. - 3:57:42 PM

4:04:26 PM - Amendment 10 - Powers of the States and People. Ratified 12/15/1791. The powers not delegated to the United States by the Constitution, nor prohibited by it to the States, are reserved to the States respectively, or to the people.

The powers delegated to the people are life , liberty and the pursuit of happiness. The powers delegated the to the state is to serve the people and defend the powers delegated to the people, life, liberty and the pursuit of happiness. So this was created after the Constitution was ratified because there were questions over who had the main power or last say, the federal government or the state government and this is saying the state has the last say, not the federal government. What this means is every single state can have their own rules and the federal government has no say because the state serves the people in that state and its purpose is to make sure it protects the peoples life, liberty and pursuit of happiness. The magic of this is each state on one hand can have totally different laws and rules than all the other states. This creates a checks and balance because every state will be trying to become more free than other states. One state on a scale of freedom is at 40% and then the state next to them has 60% freedom and so the people in the initial state will see that kind of freedom and they will pass laws to try to be as free as the 60% state. If the federal government trumps the states then every state will be the same. The United States is a creature and the creature has 50 odd cells which are states, and each cell is looking for absolute freedom so there are 50 experiments going on in the creature called the United States. Some cells become less free and some cells become more free. The goal of the states is not to see how many rules and laws they can accumulate but to see how few rules and laws they can have and still remain viable.

Amendment 16 - Status of Income Tax Clarified. Ratified 2/3/1913. The Congress shall have power to lay and collect taxes on incomes, from whatever source derived, without apportionment among the several States, and without regard to any census or enumeration.

The 16th Amendment cancels out the 10th Amendment. The 10th amendment says states get the final call above the federal government and this amendment says the federal government gets the final call above the states. If every person in a state determines their pursuit of happiness is to not pay these taxes the state must serve the people and protect their pursuit of happiness but the 16th Amendment says the state has no say, yet the states only purpose is to protect the peoples wishes in that state. So this 16th amendment is a hijacking by carpetbaggers to negate the power of the states. The people are the first priority then the state is the second and the federal government is the third in the chain and this amendment says the federal government is the first priority and the state is the second and the people are the third. So there are states trying to serve the people and the people trying to become as free as possible and then this tyrant steps in and says "States and people you do as I say," and that is tyranny. America is supposed to have fifty odd states in various states of freedom, but that is impossible if a non state steps in and says "This is how all fifty odd states are going to behave."

"The Congress shall have power to lay and collect taxes on incomes, from whatever source derived, without apportionment among the several States, and without regard to any census or enumeration." This is saying no matter what any state says ever the federal government is the bottom line and calling all the shots. It is not even relevant to the comment is about taxes because this amendment is a power grab. This comment ["The Congress shall have power to lay and collect taxes on incomes, from whatever source derived,] is usury, usury is an unfair tax or interest rate. The federal government is congress and it did not have the right to collect taxes on income and then it voted and said it did have the right. The people did not vote to allow the federal government to take their money, the federal government voted to allow their self to take the peoples' money. So the federal government in the 16th amendment cancelled out the 10th amendment and took the power from the states, and the first thing it did was vote to say it gets to take money from the people of those states. So this amendment kills the states power, and the state is suppose to protect the people, and if it doesn't then the people are fair picking for the federal government. The state is the only thing that can protect the people from the tyrant, the federal government, so the federal government kills the state and then the people are the federal government's slaves. This is slavery ""The Congress shall have power to lay and collect taxes on incomes, from whatever source derived,".

On this date the people did not have to pay the piper 2/2/1913 and on this date the people had to pay the piper 2/3/1913 because this 16th Amendment killed the states. The states answer to the federal government and because of that the people answer to the federal government and because of that the states and the people in them are no longer free or attempting to achieve absolute freedom because they are just slaves to the tyrant which is the federal government, but the federal government is not a state it is just a group of carpetbaggers. The state is real and tangible and the powerhouse to the people and where the militia's, are not the federal government. There is no militia in the federal government because the federal government is the tyrant. The tyrant is what the militia in the states is supposed to protect the people from. The fact there is no militia in the federal government proves the federal government is the tyrant.

"The tree of liberty must be refreshed from time to time with the blood of patriots and tyrants. It is it's natural manure." - Thomas Jefferson (1743–1826)

Partriot – state militia

Tyrant – federal government

The patriots should have attacked the federal government when it passed Amendment 16 but it did not so now there is tyranny and the tyrant has passed a law to give itself the people's money and the reason for that is the traditional education has made every one afraid and very mentally dull so they are just sheep wandering around in a daze. There is a tyrant stealing all the people's money and killing the states and everyone has no idea that is even happening. The 16th amendment changed our name from the United States of America to the Federal Government of America. That one is perhaps not going to go over well with the sheeple.

"That whenever any Form of Government becomes destructive of these ends, it is the Right of the People to alter or to abolish it, and to institute new Government," Declaration of Independence

{ That whenever any Form of Government} = federal government ; tyrant
[becomes destructive of these ends] = kills the states power ala 16 amendment
[it is the Right of the People to alter or to abolish it, and to institute new Government,"] = ["The tree of liberty must be refreshed from time to time with the blood of patriots and tyrants]
[it is the Right of the People to alter or to abolish it] = [It is it's natural manure.] = it has to happen or the tyrant will take over everything and lock everyone in cages. = ["The Congress shall have power to lay and collect taxes on incomes(usury tax), from whatever source derived,] = A person has to pay interest for having the privilege to work. A person is not only mentally hindered by the forced traditional education, but then they get a slave job, and they have to pay money to the ones who mentally hindered them so they can work that slave job or they will be put in jail.
I really should perhaps avoid personal commentaries. I am pleased I live in space and no one can see me or understand anything I say. Impossibility separates the courageous from the caged. Ones who are brainwashed will argue taxes are needed to fix roads but the reality is, if a state wants their roads fixed they fix them and that is not good or bad if they do not fix them. We are 50 odd states all experimenting with absolute freedom so if a state does not want to fix their roads that is their pursuit of happiness. As America is now it is not 50 odd states it is one huge state and that is uniform relative to laws, and that is not what America is supposed to be. No human being or group is ever able to define the absolute definition of pursuit of happiness so no matter what a state decides is its pursuit of happiness based on the people in that states pursuit of happiness they are never wrong. If a state's people vote and say a person can have 20 wives that is right relative to that's states pursuit of happiness. If a state says "All drugs are legal" that is right relative to that states pursuit of happiness relative to the people in that states pursuit of happiness. Once the Federal government gets involved they want every state to be identical and that destroys the states pursuit of happiness and thus the people in that states pursuit of happiness. If the people in a state vote to make all drugs illegal and television illegal that is right relative to that state pursuit of happiness. If a states people vote that everyone has to wear a moose hat that is right relative to that states pursuit of happiness. The Federal government has no right to ever tell a state what to do ever because the state is the collective conscience of the people in that state. America is not supposed to be fifty identical states it is supposed to be fifty totally different states that make up one entity called the United States of Freedom. The greatest right of a state and thus the people in that state is to be left alone. People will figure out what freedom is by their own determinations and no bully tyrant can sway them one way or another except by force or fear tactics. If one wants to be in a tyranny they can go to

84

any other country in the world but America is freedom and so it should not be anything like any other country in the world ever. America is an experiment in freedom and the only thing America is threaten by is internal tyrants and control freaks, the carpetbaggers. So the traditional education, the tyrants brand of education, is forced by law on people and that alters their perception so their thoughts are controlled and so freedom is gone before one is even ten or fourteen. That is why traditional education and laws about traditional education are not mentioned anywhere in any of the founding documents because what is good for one person is not always good for everyone in a freedom scenario, it is good in tyrannies though, one size fits all is a tyranny. One should be mindful before they go spouting off about freedom that I am embarrassed enough by their deeds as it is. - 5:11:07 PM

11:36:59 PM - The highest form of optimism is ignorance.

12/15/2009 1:50:00 AM - Rika – http://www.youtube.com/watch?v=W5yLz_Q9zaA

[Matthew 28:2 And, behold, there was a great earthquake: for the angel of the Lord descended from heaven, and came and rolled back the stone from the door, and sat upon it.]

[And, behold, there was a great earthquake] is relative to once a person applies the remedy a period later right brain unveils and their mind is near coma state because the power of right brain is so great the mind is not use to having such power so it is like a earthquake to the mind, the mind is shaken. This is an indication of how powerful right brain is once it is unveiled after being veiled.

[for the angel of the Lord descended from heaven] This is relative to once the right brain is unveiled right brain descends or the person achieves the right brain being brought to the conscious state in the mind instead of being in a subconscious state when it is veiled. So hell is when right brain, unnamable one, is veiled and when right brain is unveiled after one applies the remedy they ascend into heaven state of mind, consciousness.

[and came and rolled back the stone from the door] After one applies the remedy they understand the remedy and so they can roll back the exit from hell and they can assist others to apply the remedy and assist them in finding the exit from hell, the extreme left brain state of mind.

[and sat upon it.] Is relative to once one applies the remedy and unveils right brain for the rest of their life they will know how to assist others so they become a way out of hell, they are a key holder to the exit from hell, the left brain state, so they sit on the door which means they hold the door out of hell open and assist others to leave hell also. One might suggest one becomes a fisher of men.

This verse is a repeat of this verse [Matthew 3:16 - And Jesus, when he was baptized, went up straightway out of the water: and, lo, the heavens were opened unto him, and he saw the Spirit of God descending like a dove, and lighting upon him:]
[and, lo, the heavens were opened unto him] = [for the angel of the Lord descended from heaven]
This just means after the remedy is applied the right brain unveils a short period later and cerebrally it is very noticeable.
[heavens were opened unto him] = the mind is opened, so right and left brain occupy conscious state so one not longer has subconscious so they wear their thoughts on their sleeve, like a child does.

[Matthew 3:11 I indeed baptize you with water unto repentance: but he that cometh after me is mightier than I, whose shoes I am not worthy to bear: he shall baptize you with the Holy Ghost, and with fire:]
John was mindful his days were numbered. John was mindful Herod, civilization, was aware he was waking up people, so he was grooming is successor. Left brain influenced container, Herod was mindful of John, a right brain influenced container, and wanted to kill him as soon as possible. John was saying Jesus is far greater than me, because he knew he would be killed soon and he was mindful to keep the waking up going. If John did not denote a successor then people would not have anyone to trust to wake them up. This comment is John grooming Jesus to take his place because John knew he was about to be killed by civilization and in fact we was, so this is a predication that came to pass as a result of the intuition and pattern detection of right brain. This is similar to what Jesus did at the last supper. Jesus was fully aware when his time was up so to speak, so he was mindful to give his disciples, ones he assisted in waking up, authority figure roles. This is the pattern of this battle. Civilization does not like its slaves being woken up so when someone comes by that is very good at explaining the remedy Civilization is certain to kill them. Left brain hates right brain and so it does anything to kill right brain influenced containers. So even though these wise beings were fully aware they were going to get slaughtered from the first day, they feared not and so now we have these ancient texts because they demonstrated what fear not means, in the face of certain death. This perhaps is hard for one with an emotional capacity to understand. These wise being were not capable of being afraid at all, they were just mindful civilization was going to get them and they did their best to avoid that fate but after all, where are you going to run when civilization, the cult, is coming for your head?
When Socrates was in jail his friend offered to help him escape and Socrates said 'Where can I run?" So Socrates just drank the hemlock because civilization, left brain, does not play games when it finds someone, right brain, is waking its slaves. Left brain is miserable because it dominates the mind and makes the

mind unsound so it wants every person, container, to be miserable like it is as dominate.

It does not cost very much money to make a slave, a left brain influenced container. This is why teachers of the traditional education are not paid very much money. The traditional education is not anything but a left mind bending tool so it is not important how it is taught, just get a small child and make them learn the alphabet, A,B, C's , sequential, spell words , arrange the alphabet in sequential order, and teach them a few other sequential aspects, then throw in math, which is sequence based, 1, 2, 3, and load both down with lots of rules and short term memory exercises, a left brain trait, pop quizzes, and just do that for about eight to ten years and attach rewards for doing well at the sequencing and punishment for doing bad at it, and the get the parents to assist with the punishment , and bingo, they have a nice sedated, sequential thought based slave, susceptible to fear tactics. It is simply run of the mill brainwashing and mental conditioning. I prefer to quote my "self". - 2:37:02 AM

3:43:21 AM – When all the details are removed, right brain has random access thoughts, paradox and complexity and these traits are frightening to some people, left brain influenced ones, so they wish to avoid them, so they wish to avoid applying the remedy to unveil right brain and that is their business. But when those same people decide to veil right brain in children, right brain is going to assist said people in defeating their fear of death cerebrally or literally, and right brain is not concerned which it is. A wise man understands the difference between judgment and truth. I am mindful I am exhibiting symptoms of being manic but right brain or as you know it subconscious has random access thoughts and so I can go from calm to happy to angry in a short period but no matter what I do I always end up in neutral and what I understand is this is symptom I am not warmed up or use to having right brain, subconscious in my conscious state of mind. This is why applying the remedy to unveil right brain is something suggested to be unwise by some. What I mean is the education veils right brain and the being is essentially mentally ruined after that so if they apply the remedy it takes a long time just to adjust to sound mind again so some suggest its best not to wake people up when they have been in the extreme left brain conditioned state for a certain amount of years. Am I in absolute nirvana? Certainly. Did I accidentally apply the fear not remedy? Certainly. But I am still damaged goods because my mind was bent to the left as a child and 30 odd years later it was bent back to the middle accidentally and so one may never recover from that mentally. The good news is I am in neutral and I cannot care one way or another and so I just push on like a trooper because there is no going back. So to the ones who push this traditional education with no regards to its unwanted mental side effects on the mind of a child, you are either the cruelest bastards in the universe or you are completely insane and should be caged. I will quote "myself" on that. I am pleased you have done to your own children what you did to me. You did not defeat me though and now the worm has turned. Indeed the worm has turned.

When I talk to people in chat rooms they always say the same things other people have said to me and it is like I can anticipate what they are going to say relative to what I say almost down to the exact words. I do not perceive I am reading their mind. I perceive right brains memory has a play in it and also rights brain pattern detection. If I say traditional education bends the mind to the left the typical response is "What drugs are you on." Right brain holds all the long term memories one has for their whole life so when they are in conscious mind all memories are right up front and so one has this ocean of information at their finger tips so it appears like I have this great memory or ability to understand many concepts but really I have subconscious, right brain in my conscious state and it never forgets any concept ever.

The thing about these ancient texts is they are certainly revolutionary against the ones who push the traditional education. Many assume these being were peaceful, namely Jesus.

That is not even in the ball park of accuracy

[Luke 12:51 Suppose ye that I am come to give peace on earth? I tell you, Nay; but rather division:]

You perceive these wise beings were going to stand by and allow children to be mentally raped?

[Luke 12:53 The father shall be divided against the son, and the son against the father; the mother against the daughter, and the daughter against the mother; the mother in law against her daughter in law, and the daughter in law against her mother in law.]

I accidentally applied the remedy and everyone I know does not believe me and they in turn still support the mental rape of children so I stand against them.

[and the son against the father;].

Jesus was against Joseph because Joseph did not believe him that is very obvious but Joseph was his father. It is not important if you believe all that sequential left brain education mentally bends a small child's mind to the left, because ignorance is no excuse. If you support and allow that "brand" of education to be forced on children I stand against you and I will assist you in understanding what stand against means. There are essentially only two kinds of humans left on this planet after all these years of traditional education. Insane people who are very afraid and insane people who are fearless and vengeful, and both despise each other. If you perceive the ones who have applied the remedy do not despise the ones who have not applied the remedy you are clinically out of touch with reality. Do you despise people who rape small children? That is good because I despise them also, and I despise people who mentally rape small children infinitely more whether they know not what they do or whether they know what they do. A shrink once told me it is best to get your thoughts down on a piece of paper. I f"nd that quite amusing at this point because "erhaps they should have also mentioned (But under no circumstance publish them.) You would be infinitely wise to not underestimate this comment [John 15:13 Greater love hath no man than this, that a man lay down his life for his friends(children).]

"Always do right. This will gratify some people and astonish the rest."- Mark Twain.

Perhaps his definition of do right was hide. Always hide. You will gratify yourself and astonish the rest.- 4:42:41 AM

5:16:06 AM – I am mindful before the accident I was very depressed and suicidal for over ten years and in fact I was suicidal at about the age of fourteen which means I spend a very long time mindful in that 9th circle of hell, treason and I am mindful that means my metal is very strong. I accidentally applied this ancient remedy and now I am not depressed and suicidal. I will finish my infinite books and perhaps ones who come after you will be able to understand what I write about. - 5:18:11 AM

6:02:22 AM — [Luke 23:12 And the same day Pilate and Herod were made friends together: for before they were at enmity between themselves.] So Herod cut off Johns head and then Pilate and Herod become friends and then they understand they must k"ll Jesus because Je"us is John the Baptists successor. So Herod and Pilate represent the (powers that be) or the rulers in civilization, rulers of the left brain influenced containers, relative to this area of the world and time period. This verse is relative to this verse.
[Psalms 2:2 The kings of the earth set themselves, and the rulers take counsel together, against the LORD, and against his anointed, saying, [Psalms 2:3 Let us break their bands asunder, and cast away their cords from us.]
Kings of the earth is relative to the ones in extreme left brain state after they get the education relative to [Genesis 1:1 In the beginning God created the heaven and the earth.] So earth is left brain and heaven is right brain. So Kings of the earth are ones in extreme left brain and kings of heaven are ones who apply the remedy after getting traditional education and are Lords or Masters.
[and the rulers take counsel together] = [And the same day Pilate and Herod were made friends together] So what this is suggesting is a conspiracy. The rulers of the "earth" understood these beings were waking up their slaves and so they wanted to stop them. [Let us break their bands asunder] this is relative to divide and conquer. This is perhaps why Jesus told his disciples to spread out so that if they were caught they would only catch one at a time not the whole group. This is why the disciples were killed in different places and this is why they went to various countries because the written language was in every country so every country conditioned people in extreme left brain. Again the deeper reality is left brain influenced containers hate right brain influenced containers and seek to kill them because they will make everyone right brain influenced containers and left brain does not want to come back into the fold of mental harmony because then it is reduced to second fiddle.
This comment is relative to the Kinds of heaven, the ones who apply the remedy.

[Jeremiah 51:57 And I will make drunk her princes, and her wise men, her captains, and her rulers, and her mighty men: and they shall sleep a perpetual sleep, and not wake, saith the King, whose name is the LORD of hosts.]

One conditioned into the extreme left brain by traditional education is slothful in their thoughts and they are what is called in these texts the dead relative to the quick and the dead. Another way to look at it is [drunk her princes, and her wise men, her captains, and her rulers, and her mighty men] they are drunk as in mentally unsound or insane. And that is the same as saying [and they shall sleep a perpetual sleep, and not wake]. So they are mentally asleep or hindered. And the c'mment they will not wake is relative to it "s hard for"a rich man to enter the kingdom and it is relative to Dante+s first circle of hell (limbo) where a rich person is the farthest from the 9th circle of hell where the exit to hell is, treason. So"all of the"e people listed are the rich relative to the reverse world or relative to the rulers of (earth). Princes, wise men, captains, rulers and mighty men. The comment [1 Corinthians 3:18 Let no man deceive himself. If any man among you seemeth to be wise in this world, let him become a fool, that he may be wise.] All of these beings Princes, wise men, captains, rulers and mighty men think they are wise relative to the ones conditioned into the left brain state of mind; their cup is full so they cannot be taught truth. They perceive they are wise because they have the education but in reality they are mentally hindered. So this verse is relative to the reverse thing.[let him become a fool, that he may be wise.] One can only get out of the mental hell caused by the traditional education by humiliation and that is the 9th circle of hell, treason. That is relative to saying perhaps a lot, listening to music one dislikes, and of course defeating ones fear of death. Those things all appear foolish to ones conditioned into left brain but they are the key to escaping mental hell and unveiling right brain and becoming wise. One has to humiliate their self to the point of mental treason to escape mental hell, left brain state, and that appears foolish, but only to fools. - 6:32:30 AM

8:38:54 AM – Letter to someone about something

First the accident: I was depressed for many years and fourteen months ago I took a handful of pills and I became very ill and my mind told me I would die if i did not call for help and then I decided I will not call for help.

I accidentally applied the ancient remedy.

[Luke 17:33 ; and whosoever shall lose his life shall preserve it.]

About one month later I got this extreme mental "ah ha" sensation. I lost my sense of time and it was very difficult mentally for me. About two months after that I became compelled to write books and I started to write books about the ancient texts.

I have published 13 books explaining the ancient texts since then.

The "ah ha" sensation happened on Oct 31st at 1:38 PM. So the solution to the riddle "No man knows the hour or day but the father" is.

No man knows the hour or day of an accident but the father of the accident. Oct 31st at 1:38 PM.

I am mindful the tree of knowledge is written language and math. Neurologically speaking Written language is based on sequence.

A, B , C. Spelling is arranging letters in sequence. Sentence structure is also arranging words in sequence. Sequence is a left brain trait so after a child gets a few years of this their mind bends to the left and so after the education their mind is like a crescent moon, very strong left brain and veiled right brain.

Jesus spoke about suffer the children and that is relative to the scribes or Sadducee's giving the children the traditional education instead of oral education and that is relative to this comment [Luke 17:2 It were better for him that a millstone were hanged about his neck, and he cast into the sea, than that he should offend one of these little ones.]

. [than that he should offend one of these little ones.] = veiling a child's mind with written education and leaving the child in a state of mental suffering known as hell.

As explained in Genesis

[Genesis 3:6 And when the woman saw that the tree was good for food, and that it was pleasant to the eyes, and a tree to be desired to make one wise, she took of the fruit thereof, and did eat, and gave also unto her husband with her; and he did eat.}

Written education looks good to gain wisdom, the letters and script are pleasing to the eyes and written education is thought or desired to make one wise.

Neurologically speaking.

After one gets all this sequential left brain education their fear and emotions such as shame, greed, lust, envy increase because their mind is bent to the left and this affects the hypothalamus and is also relative to the fact when right brain is veiled ones mind is slothful, or sequential based thoughts, so thoughts such as fear and lust and greed can be maintained for long periods unlike when right brain is unveiled.

So before one eats off the tree of knowledge, gets the written education

[Genesis 2:25 And they were both naked, the man and his wife, and were not ashamed.]

One is not exhibiting shame and fear or embarrassment

and after one gets the written education

[Genesis 3:10 And he said, I heard thy voice in the garden, and I was afraid, because I was naked; and I hid myself.]

One becomes afraid and self conscious because their mind is unsound and they start having lots of fear relative to :[2 Timothy 1:7 For God hath not given us the spirit of fear; but of power, and of love, and of a sound mind.]

So spirit of fear is caused by the written education, tree of knowledge and so it means one has an unsound mind because this spirit of fear [and I was afraid, because I was naked; and I hid myself.] is not of God so it is ungodly.[For God hath not given us the spirit of fear]

So this comment [Mark 3:29 But he that shall blaspheme against the Holy Ghost hath never forgiveness, but is in danger of eternal damnation:} Means anyone who gives this written education will veil the right brain, relative to God made man in his image, and in turn [blaspheme against the Holy Ghost].

Neurologically speaking since this left brain extreme state caused by the written language causes much fear because if affects the hypothalamus [[2 Timothy 1:7 For God hath not given us the spirit of fear] [and I was afraid, because I was naked; and I hid myself.] The remedy is fear not relative to [Genesis 15:1 After these things the word of the LORD came unto Abram in a vision, saying, Fear not, Abram: I am thy shield, and thy exceeding great reward.]

[Fear not, Abram: I am thy shield, and thy exceeding great reward.] = [Tho i walk through the shadow of death I fear (not) no evil) = [[Luke 17:33 ; and whosoever shall lose his life shall preserve it.] = Abraham held the knife over Isaac after he bound Isaac and Isaac was not aware Abraham would not kill him because Isaac asked Abraham , where is the sheep you are going to sacrifice. So when Isaac did not run he feared not, or did not try to save himself so he preserved it, or thought he was going to die, walked through the valley of the shadow of death and he feared not or Issac perceived death and submitted to it and neurologically speaking this shocks the hypothalamus back into working properly and this unveiled the right brain and one returns to sound mind. So one has to deny their self, self being one after they get written education, relative to [Matthew 16:24 Then said Jesus unto his disciples, If any man will come after me, let him deny himself, and take up his cross, and follow me.]

[let him deny himself]

So if one is in a situation they perceive certain death, but in reality it can be the shadow of death, and they fear not, they deny their self, or they tell the hypothalamus they will no longer listen to it.

So when i took those pills my hypothalamus said you will die and I feared not, or I denied myself and that one second mental decision negated the left brain extreme state of mind the written education put me in, so I unveiled right brain and lost my sense of time because right brain has lots of ambiguity, so when I try to think how much time has passed my mind says infinite time has passed and d no time has passed and that is its final answer so I cannot tell how much time has passed.

Relative to [1 John 2:18 Little children, it is the last time: and as ye have heard that antichrist shall come, even now are there many anti-christs; whereby we know that it is the last time.]

John is telling the children to beware of the scribes who will push this written education on them and harm them. There are many anti-christ's relates to the fact everyone get the written education. This is relative to why Jesus spoke orally or was an orator and did not write.

Antichrist is relative to [Luke 20:46 Beware of the scribes, which desire to walk in long robes, and love greetings in the markets, and the highest seats in the synagogues, and the chief rooms at feasts;]

Scribes = Ones who get the written education.

Blessed are the poor in spirit is relative to the meek shall inherit the earth

Meek is ones who are depressed relative to "the world" or reverse world because they are near the 9th circle of hell relative to Dante's Inferno, treason, relative to. Tho i walk through the valley of the shadow of death I fear not or commit treason or deny ones self.

The ones in "the world'" who are in the 1st circle of hell are in limbo because they are further away from the 9th circle of hell, and the exit from hell , the left brain extreme state caused by written language is there,

Relative to one has to go through hell to get to heaven. So the depressed and suicidal are in the treason level of the mental hell so they have a chance to escape.

Socrates suggested , no true philosopher fears death and that is relative to though i walk through the valley of the shadow of death I do not fear death and he was killed because he was corrupting the mind of the youth, he was telling them the written language was harming them. He said suffer the children to much, so to speak. END

8:46:14 AM - When one see's failure as understanding they are only left with success. When drowning stop breathing. Failing to succeed keeps one occupied.

4:43:03 PM – Sometimes the eyes suggest light when the intuition suggests otherwise. Sometimes safety is unsafe. Some go to great lengths to escape to nothing. Being zero for six billion has no down side.

12/16/2009 2:34:55 AM – The concept of belief relative to these ancient texts is about one thing only. Do you believe that written language you were taught as a child bent your mind to the left? Written language is sequence based and left brain is sequenced based so do you believe that education bent your mind to the left? If one cannot get that far in their thought processes relative to cause and effect relationships relative to written language they are what is known as, in eternal damnation, mentally. They are the lost that will never be found. This reality is not a symptom of person's intelligence it is a symptom of how devastating this left brain state is on the mind. There are no human beings on this planet who have not applied this remedy after getting the traditional education that can possibly pose a threat to a human being who has applied the remedy, mental faculties relative. That is an indication of how powerful right brain is. The quick and the dead mentally speaking. Once one applies the remedy they are only able to use extremes to explain the contrast between before they applied the remedy and after they applied the remedy. Some suggest light and dark. Some suggest lost then found. Some suggest quick and dead. Some suggest resurrected from the dead. The accurate way to look at it is a child is mentally sound then they get the traditional education and then their mind is bent to the left and then they apply the remedy and go back to sound mind but then they cannot use written language relative to how civilization considers using written language properly and that is the proof written language is a conditioning mind altering tool. One might suggest if you can spell well you can't think well. That is the trade off. Do you want to have a mind as sharp as a tack or do you want to arrange letters in sequential order well, so your friends will boast about how wise you are for exhibiting said spelling ability. I do not mind not being able to use the written language because I am only talking to myself anyway. I am mindful I am not actually using written language as a pretext to write books I am in fact attempting to translate cerebral thoughts into words and I am fully aware I cannot do that to any kind of satisfaction so I just keep trying. I cannot fully translate the cerebral thoughts and I also cannot spell cerebral thoughts wrong. Every time I type certain words like cerebral I misspell it and get the letters out of order so I just use the spell checker so my ability to use the written language is gone relative to and English teachers ability to use written language. A better way to look at it is this remedy negates the effects caused by the written education conditioning and so after one applies it they can no longer use written language they learned, so this remedy negates what the education did mentally to a person. If you want to be an author do not apply the remedy. If you want to write infinite books don't apply the remedy.

X = acceptability by peers because one can use written language
Y = insulted by peers because one cannot use written language
Z = sound mind
A = unsound mind
X = A
Y = Z

So civilization puts a person in a situation that if they want to be accepted by their peers they have to pay the piper by sacrificing their mind. This of course is reality but I am mindful ones who have no applied the remedy are completely unaware of that reality. One may be praised for their written language ability but I can assure them it costs them their sound mind, so it perhaps is not worth it to some. If you want someone to praise you for your sequencing ability it will cost you your random access mental ability. If you want to be a great intellect it will cost you your intuition mental ability. If you want to be very linear it will cost you your pattern detection mental ability. What the remedy does is bring one back to the middle so they have a little of all of these aspects. A little bit of sequencing and random access for example. It is important to understand I was very adept at written language before the accident. The accident was a mental process so I did not lose my ability to use written language because of a physiological event. Einstein was certainly awake or right brain unveiled to a degree and what is interesting is he did poorly in school which is why he did work at a patient office. The pattern there is some people do not take well to the traditional education in fact Einstein was not good at math and even with his discoveries and theories he made up his own symbols for math. I did not become right brain dominate because of this accident. In reality I got traditional education and my mind bent to the left and then I accidentally applied this ancient remedy and went back to the middle and so I exhibit right brain and left brain traits which is expected in a sound mind. Because of this people who are bent to the left as a result of the education confuse me at times. One might suggest it is difficult communicating with mentally unsound beings. The first symptom of a sane mind is it questions if it is insane. Early after the accident I was certain I went insane because I could not relate to anyone I was talking to and I was attacking everyone I was talking to. I still do some attacking but at first I attacked everyone. I assumed it was me who had the problem because I was not aware what had happened or what this accident meant. I thought I was insane because I could not imagine I became sane, and everyone else I was talking to essentially was insane, of unsound mind because they did not apply the ancient remedy to the "tree of knowledge". Insane people do not question if they are insane, and that is proof they are insane. Ambiguity of right brain was making me question if I was insane shortly after the accident. I had many moments of doubt but because right brain is so good at pattern detection and intuition it only took me about a year relative to calendar to sort it all out. It may hurt your feelings when I suggest if you got that written education and did not apply the remedy in one form or another you are clinically insane and clinically of unsound mind, but the truth oft assists one in questioning what they should do about it. It is too late to wish away the past and wish you never got the traditional education. You got that education and I know you did because I got it so the next step is to be pleased these wise beings from our past figured out how to correct the mental imbalance caused by the traditional education. So these wise beings were looking out for us and they knew it was a very good chance we would get the traditional education so they went ahead and explained the remedy. Once a person applies the remedy to the full measure the ancient texts perhaps can no longer assist a person so they are only of value to the ones who have not applied the remedy. Once one applies the remedy that being is what the ones who wrote the ancient texts were. All the ancient texts are is the cause, tree of knowledge, the effects, unsound mind, beast, full of fear state of mind, mental suffering, and the remedy, fear not, deny ones self. So one understands the tree of knowledge, one understand the mental effects of getting the tree of knowledge and one applies the remedy to getting the tree of knowledge and then there is nothing else to talk about, so go live your life with a sound mind and attempt to learn your lesson about what some of mankind's inventions can do to the mind if they are not respected and taught properly. That's the lesson of the ancient texts. Mankind is so intelligent he is capable of inventing things that appear to be a good idea but can actually have unintended consequences. Mankind used his powerful mind and powerful creativity of right brain to invent written language and in learning written language it in fact veiled right brain and silenced mankind's creativity, so mankind could not find a way to get out of that state of mind because it requires pattern detection and intuition which are right brain traits and they were also veiled by the written language invention created using right brain traits. So perhaps you are asking yourself then what are we all killing each other for over the religious texts and the answer is because you are of unsound mind. A better way to look at it is if the beings from the ancient texts were here they would all be on the same side but the ones who read those texts and have not applied the remedy are in left brain and they only see the ancient texts as parts, separate parts, and so they fight each other because they do not have the mental ability to understand they are killing each other to defend each other's doctrines.

95

Religions:

Remedy to tree of knowledge.

X = fear not, face shadow of death and fear not

Y = deny ones self , lose one's life to preserve it, get dunked under water until you are afraid and then fear not

Z = submit(to perceived death)

A = sit in a cemetery alone at night until you feel better

So if any of these religions fight each other they are fights over pure vanity because they are all saying the same doctrine. And if anyone does not understand that, it is proof they have not applied the remedy in the ancient texts. Four people who all have the exact same belief killing each other because they do not mentally understand they all have the same belief, and that can only happen in an insane asylum. So when a person of one of these doctrine systems insults a person of another doctrine system, they are in fact actually insulting their own belief system. One might suggest they know not what they do. The deeper problem is the ones who get the education are of unsound mind and are prone to be violent. Simply put a person with right brain unveiled tends to fights their battles mentally and one who has right brain veiled only has the physical battle to fight. Relative to the wars in the ancient texts the ones who applied the remedy had to use self control to become violent and the ones who did not apply the remedy had to use self control to avoid becoming violent. That is the difference between a nervous wreck and a calm being. This concept is also relative to patience. I am mindful I cannot convince civilization to stop doing what it does to children mentally with its current system of education but right brain keeps telling me "Wait until I get warmed up to at least 1% before you make any physical moves to solve this situation." I am mindful I am trying to do the impossible with words and right brain would not have it any other way because it only deals with the impossible. Left brain deals with all the possible tasks and right brain takes on the impossible tasks. It sounds very supernatural but the truth is right brain gets better when it perceives impossibility. All problems are relative to solutions and right brain ponders so fast, only problems with vast complexity and the appearance of impossibility even get its attention. Right brain has stripped all the details relative to the recorded history of mankind and found the core problem and the core solution and it did it in one year or less and now it is simply attempting to explain it in infinite ways to solve that problem. Right brain will be displeased if it solves that problem because it understands there is no other problem or all other problems go back to this one problem. No matter how egotistical I may sound I am always going to remind you it is not me it is right brain. I am in fact an accident going along for the ride. Everything is downhill once we as a species address the unwanted mental side effects of these manmade inventions called written language and math. If you ignore the spirit of what I suggest about these inventions all that is going to do is guarantee right brain is going to get better at explaining it because right brain does not understand what loss or win is, it is just an experimenter. Perhaps that's not even a word. I do not perceive I am exhibiting any mental effort at all in writing these texts and I have no fatigue or ability to think about what I am going to say next and that is an indication of how powerful right brain when unveiled is. Think about the equation e= mc2. This is getting energy from matter and if we split the proper atoms we can get lots of energy from those atoms but if that energy output is compared to the energy output of right brain when it is unveiled there is no comparison. If one could capture a thought and measure it and then measure the thought processing power of right brain when unveiled, and contrast that with the splitting of an atom relative to energy output, it would be a no contest. Right brain is so powerful when unveiled I cannot even explain how powerful it is and I have it unveiled so it is beyond my understanding but I prefer to say it is the machine. Even in chat rooms when I speak I type thoughts so fast people say "That's a bot" as in robot. People ask me in chat rooms "Where are you copying and pasting that stuff from?" So even to human beings who do not have right brain unveiled I appear like a machine. I am not a machine we are machines and the reason the tribes in the Amazon just sit around apparently and take it easy is because there are no problems they have not already solved, that are solvable. Civilization could solve all of it's problems in perhaps less than five years if it started unveiling right brain and then it would find out we as a species are too intelligent and find out perhaps we invented written language to make ourselves mentally numb to make life a challenge, because life was not a challenge. That sounds like a right brain ideal. Right brain wants impossible challenges so it can exercise, so right brain creativity created written language and in turn that silenced right brain so what was flat ground relative to problems now appears to be mountains. So everything looks like impossibility to ones who have not applied the remedy after getting traditional education but in reality on a deep psychological species collective level we all have purpose as a result because when right brain was unveiled before written education life was so easy we had no purpose at all.

So perhaps we are a species that nature made way to intelligent and besides looking for food, we all have no purpose. One can take a simple job that is boring and make it a complex job that is challenging but in reality it is still a simple job. We took a simple purposeless existence and with our extreme intelligence turned it into a complex purposeful existence but in reality it is still a simple purposeless existence. People are born and then they die. If one wants to create a million details and complexity to get to that end conclusion that gives the impression of purpose and meaning but in reality it is simply being born and then dying. Flatten all your tires and drive to work. Your ride to work will have lots of meaning and purpose, but you still end up at work. A species without purpose would logically attempt to create the illusion of purpose. Perhaps having no purpose is the greatest fear of all relative to mankind. Other animals are a bit less intelligent or aware so they are just under the radar of mentally being able to understand they have no purpose. So then homo-sapiens come along and have a large brain and achieve the level of intelligence to become aware they have no purpose and so they counter act that devastating awareness by numbing their self down mentally. I am mindful I am not insulting any human being I am attempting to explain how intelligent we are, and perhaps if one applies the remedy they will become aware

97

of this no purpose reality and it will perhaps harm them. Perhaps this heightened awareness of no purpose harmed us so much we choose to become ignorant and invented something to make us ignorant to this no purpose reality unknowingly or subconsciously on a deep mental level. If one suggests to another person we have no purpose that person will perhaps rattle off many reasons we certainly do have purpose but only because they would never want to mentally understand they have no purpose. In the machine state of mind no purpose is a purpose because in the machine state one has few emotions so something like no purpose is just a word and no purpose is relative to nothing and relative to loss of attachment and that does not mean anything to a machine because a machine is in the now. No purpose denotes future expectations but in the now, in the machine state one has no ability to grasp future expectations. I can suggest a host of things I want to do tomorrow but I have no expectations about tomorrow so when tomorrow gets here I will have forgotten those expectations, and anticipation is relative to emotions. In the machine state one has no emotional capacity so a comment like "I can't wait until the weekend" does not mean anything in the machine state because without emotions one cannot understand what "I can't wait" means. "I can't wait" denotes emotions such as excitement and thus anticipation of excitement. When one has all those emotions in that left brain state they create situations so they can feel all those emotions. In the machine state the very definition of fun is not possible and love is not possible and hate is not possible on any kind of time duration that one in the left brain state could relate to. My mind cannot tell what depression is or happiness is so those words were invented to express mental symptoms of one who has been conditioned into the extreme left brain state. Depression is sloth and happiness is lust. Depression is envy and happiness is greed. - 5:05:20 AM

5:33:41 AM — [Genesis 1:2 And the earth was without form, and void; and darkness was upon the face of the deep .]
[Genesis 2:17 But of the tree of the knowledge of good and evil, thou shalt not eat of it: for in the day that thou eatest thereof thou shalt surely die.]
[without form, and void] = no purpose
[But of the tree of the knowledge of good and evil] = contrast = purpose
So the above comments are saying once we had no purpose and then we did something to give us the illusion of purpose. There is one group of people explaining how much better they are than another group of people and so that perceived contrast or seeing things as parts gives them purpose. Trying to convince someone to be like you is a form of purpose but it is also a form of vanity because they are already like you in one respect. The tribes in the Amazon are not trying to convince civilization to be like them but civilization is trying to "assist" the tribes in the Amazon to be like they are. So this is an ego trip relative to civilization. Civilization wants to help the tribes in the Amazon that are just fine and have lived in harmony for thousands of years longer than civilization has been around and the funny thing is civilization is certain beyond a shadow of a doubt it is wiser than those tribes in the Amazon. If a tribe from the Amazon came to America and lived in the wild some concerned citizen would see them in the wild and call the

police and the police would take their children away under the guise of protecting the children from the parents and at the same time the parents in civilization send their kids to a factory to get their minds bent to the left and the police do not say a word about that. Civilization is a lunatic asylum with lunatics running around try to assist the sane people, children, to become lunatics. Civilization has a monetary system and that is proof they are lunatics because the tribes in the Amazon do not need money because they have sound minds and a sound mind can keep one going and supply ones needs because a sound mind is very powerful. Now civilization has raped the land and destroyed all the natural food supplies and this means they have a strangle hold on the food supply and only people with money can buy their food and to top it off the left brain conditioning makes ones hunger so great, they have to eat three meals a day just to have any brain function at all. The ones who have been conditioned actually become weak if they do not eat three meals a day and that is hilarious because I have never experienced a being hallucinating to that degree. A human being gets weak if they do not eat for one day and that is proof something is seriously wrong with that human beings mind where it would tell them they are weak and tired and cannot concentrate if they do not eat for one day. One day without food and that person's body is starting to show symptoms of near death experience. You know when your stomach growls and you feel weak and say "I need to get something to eat soon." That is a hallucination caused by your mind being bent so far to the left it is sending you false signals and you are certain they are not hallucinations or delusions. I suppose I could just stop eating for five days to see how that would affect my thinking, or my thoughts, or the metal clarity when right brain is unveiled but I risk the chance I may become enlightened and I certainly do not want to risk that. Ignorance is not stupidity and has no bearing on intelligence. Ignorance is simply the right brain being veiled and the intuition and pattern detection and lightening processing speed is silenced. If a person shoots a drug into their brain that turns off the left and right hemisphere then they will understand how intelligent they were when they only had the left brain working so they will have a contrast. Then if a person applies the remedy and unveils right brain they will again have a contrast to how they were with right brain veiled and how they are with right brain unveiled. Wisdom is simply the point at which a human being negates the mental side effects of the written education by unveiling right brain. So a wise man is a person who is mentally sound and nothing more and nothing special. Mentally sound is how everyone is born so it impossible it could be special or unique. Then the traditional education bends the mind to the left and makes one mentally unsound. Then a person has purpose and for the rest of their life they try to go back to being mentally sound. One is not really accomplishing anything by applying the remedy relative to the fact if they did not get the traditional education they would not have to apply the remedy. One is born on square zero and then they get the traditional education and get thrown back to square negative one and then they apply the remedy and they go back to square zero. So the illusion of purpose is achieved through vanity. There are many who spend their whole life trying to reach square zero and that is purpose relative to giving them the illusion of progression. One cannot go any further beyond square zero, sound mind. At square zero one loses purpose because unveiling right brain, the machine, means one loses emotional capacity. I am mindful this no purpose reality is dark but the trick is to be mindful there is no purpose and then take one step back and the first thing that one perceives is important is ones purpose. Purpose to many is relative to emotions. In order to have purpose one has to achieve goals and if those goals are reached one feels the emotional satisfaction and if the goals are not reached one feels the emotion dissatisfaction. Right brain cannot sense satisfaction or dissatisfaction because it is pondering to too fast to maintain any mental state of emotions. Ones with emotions may perceive that is sad but sad is also an emotion so they are emotional based on every level and can only relate to things on an emotional scale because in the left brain bent mindset all the mind has is an infinite supply of strong emotions and that is a symptom concentration, complexity, intuition and thus heightened awareness is hindered. Some will argue that everybody needs love and everybody needs fear but those emotions are not love or fear they are symptoms of attachment. Dante said it the best when he said in Paradiso, XVII (55-60) "how hard a path it is for one who goes ascending and descending others' stairs". The mind bent to the left is a slave to its own emotions and a slave to the emotions of others around them. The only way escape the stairs is the machine state or neutral and that is a sound mind, when right brain is unveiled. One is either going to be a slave to making sure they do not upset the emotions of the unsound beings, or they are a slave and censor of their own thoughts. One may not say what is on their mind to make sure they do not upset the beings with their emotions turned up so then they have determined their thoughts are best kept silenced. If someone with their mind bent to the left so they have vast emotions gets upset by anything, I suggest that is their burden and their suffering because the wise beings told them the remedy to that mental state thousands of years ago so apparently those beings who get emotional over words must like suffering to begin with. If someone throws you a life preserver and you swim away from it your certainly must like drowning and I am pleased to observe you are pleased to drown. If you desire to not apply the remedy I will be pleased to write books into infinity explaining how much you love suffering. A masochist is a person with a tendency to invite and enjoy misery of any kind in order to be pitied by others or admired for forbearance. [admired for forbearance.]

Admired for forbearance is essentially the definition of civilization. Civilization bends the children's mind to the left and then explains how well it does at dealing with all the problems created as a result of bending everyone's mind to the left. That is also called a self harmer and I understand self harming because I use to be a Master at it. I moved on to the next stage which is called indifference and that is very mentally healthy especially when one finds their self in a lunatic asylum. I do not need to hear a masochist explain to me the dangers of indifference. Only a masochist fears indifference. The power of indifference is it drives masochists out of their mind. I learned one important lesson through my years of self harming and that is I can harm myself much greater than the universe can ever harm me and that means I am indifferent to you because you pose absolutely no threat to me in contrast to myself. The only way to deal with a rabid animal is either kill it or be indifferent to it. I imagine being a masochist is as good a profession as any considering the location. So I am mindful you fully understand the remedy and I am mindful you perhaps have grown quite attached to being a masochist. One does not have to worry about the other masochists because if one has not applied they remedy, they are the greatest masochist they know. This remedy has been around for thousands of years and if you still have not applied it then it is best you get a tattoo on your forehead that says ' I love suffering and I am a master Masochist." to go along with that other mark you have, and then you can hope the job market for master masochists opens up. One in this extreme left brain state of mind is really a Sadomasochist and that is not worse than a masochist it is simply different. A masochist harms their self to feel good and a sadomasochist harms others to feel good but that is not really accurate either, to explain the "sane". I say "I " way to much because some being after the accident said "Do not say I way too much." When I do not say the word I that is proof I have self control. I am mindful my train of thought fell off the tracks. There is a comment I read in an Islamic chat room and I am uncertain if it was from the Quran and I am unable to reproduce the exact words but the spirit of it was "Do not always tell them knowledge because they get bored easily." It is a complex truth that one has to be serious but also be funny because the sane are cranky and they are cranky because they are suffering. If I tell too many jokes you will think I am a comedian and if I get to serious you will think I am wise. When everything is removed the spirit of what I suggest is relative to mentally hindering the minds of mentally sound innocent children so in that respect I am deadly serious. On the other hand as a species we are so intelligent we invented something that mentally hindered our own minds so we are a deadly threat to ourselves because we are too intelligent, and that is hilarious. We are so intelligent we our own worst enemy and no matter what we do we cannot ever escape that. We can make ourselves mentally hindered and we are still a threat to ourselves or we can reach sound mind and we are still a threat to ourselves. I cannot be a greater threat to you than you are to you. Our species cannot be a greater threat to anything but our species. In one way our vast intelligence is our greatest flaw and at the same time our vast intelligence is our greatest strength. It is perhaps the ultimate paradox. If we were any more intelligent we would kill our self off unknowingly but in fact we are killing our self off unknowingly so we cannot be any more intelligent. We are so intelligent we harm our self because we lose track of how powerful our intelligence is and there is no other animal on the planet that can claim that. What is hilarious about that is traditional education is attempting to make people more intelligent, but we cannot be any more intelligent, so all traditional education can possibly do is make people less intelligent and it does that flawlessly. We factually invented written language and math and that requires vast intelligence to accomplish because no other creature has ever done that, and those inventions altered our minds and made us less intelligent. We are perhaps beyond our own understanding. Our intelligence in fact has the ability to harm us if we are not mindful of it. - 12/16/2009 6:19:08 PM

11:46:13 PM - [Galatians 4:10 Ye observe days, and months, and times, and years.]

Ye = ones who get the written language and have their minds bent to the left and do not apply the fear not remedy.
This verse is simply explaining the mind senses time and that is a form of suffering. There are some comments that speak of "one day is like a thousand years."
The complexity of that is when one applies the fear not remedy and right brain is unveiled the paradox of right brain always gives the answer to "how much time has passed" as infinite time has passed and no time has passed. So the ones with right brain veiled sense time and the ones who apply the remedy and unveil right brain have no sense of time. This no sense of time is what is known as the fountain of youth. The mind itself no longer registers time because the ambiguity of right brain can never make up its mind how much time has passed.
This observation of time is relative, proven in holidays. Civilization, which is what is known as the cult of the serpent in the ancient texts celebrates holidays in order to celebrate the fact they defeated the wise beings who suggested the written language was of the serpent.
John the Baptists was not killed because he was saying he believes in God he was killed because he was waking up people who were mentally put to sleep by civilization which used this written language to veil peoples right brain, and make them sequential based in thoughts and susceptible to fear tactics.

[Matthew 3:7 But when he saw many of the Pharisees and Sadducees come to his baptism, he said unto them, O generation of vipers, who hath warned you to flee from the wrath to come?]

John attacked the ones who encouraged the written education. Pharisees were for oral law but they could read and the Sadducees were for written law. So both of these types of people got the education. One cannot read unless one learns how to write and one cannot write unless one learns the alphabet so no matter what if one gets that amount of sequencing to be able to read they have to apply the fear not remedy.
So all of these wise being were attacking civilization because it was pushing this sequential heavy invention of people and veiling their right brain and so Moses attacked civilization to free the people from the "taskmaster" or the brainwasher called civilization.

[Revelation 17:13 These have one mind, and shall give their power and strength unto the beast.]

One mind means one gets the education and veils their right brain so they are left with the sequential slothful left brain and so their powerhouse, complex right brain is veiled so they are of unsound mind and thus a beast in contrast to a sound minded being. This is relative to the comment the quick and the dead.

If one has their right brain veiled they are slothful mentally so they are the dead and then one applies the fear not remedy and they are the quick, mentally because right brain has unnameable power.

Jesus said about a woman who was going to be stoned 'Let those without sin cast the first stone" He was explaining let those who have applied the remedy judge that woman because if one applies the "those who lose their life mentally will preserve it", unveil right brain, they will be mindful the education is what put that women in a state of mind she exhibits that sin, mental symptoms.

Simply put, greed is a mental symptom one has been conditioned into left brain and so they can maintain that mental state of greed for long periods, same as lust, and envy, and pride. Right brain after being unveiled as a result of applying the remedy is pondering so fast one simply cannot remain in the state of greed or lust or envy or sloth, for more than a few seconds relative to a clock. This is relative to how powerful right brain is, one cannot maintain, lust or greed, or depression or happiness emotions for more than a few seconds before they ponder their self into another mindset. So sadness cannot be maintained and so Jesus said let the dead (ones who have not applied the remedy) bury the dead. Other words the dead cry over spilt milk from a leaking container because their mind is slothful because it has been conditioned into extreme left brain state as a result of the tree of knowledge.

So civilization idolizes these wise being with its holidays, celebrating the fact it killed the truth and hung itself in the process.

Saint Patrick said; The church is a place to heal the sick not a museum for the saints. I clarify that comment by saying the church is a place to assist ones to apply the fear not , deny ones self remedy to the tree of knowledge not a place to idolize the ones who have applied that remedy.

Perhaps if the ones who do not mind making money off their friends who have been mentally raped by the cult, and if ones do not mind watching the children continue to get mentally raped by the cult, civilization, and they can live with their self, they are infinitely wiser than I will ever be. - 12:23:22 AM

[Psalms 74:10 O God, how long shall the adversary reproach? shall the enemy blaspheme thy name for ever?]

This is a rhetorical question similar to how Moses mentioned his anger waxed hot. [Exodus 32:19 And it came to pass, as soon as he came nigh unto the camp, that he saw the calf, and the dancing: and Moses' anger waxed hot, and he cast the tables out of his hands, and brake them beneath the mount.]

Of course anger relative to the sane is not possible for ones who apply the remedy. It is more like a positive thing because the right brain is aware it cannot win so it tries even harder. This is why many of the wise beings got slaughtered because they never gave up until they were silenced by the cult, civilization.

[how long shall the adversary reproach?] How long will the ones with their mind bent all the way to the left insult the ones who break free of that brainwashing? How long will left brain revolt against right brain and try to run the mind by itself? Forever and ever perhaps because left brain is jealous of right brain and knows in a 50/50 contest, mental harmony, right brain will always get the glory, so to speak. The sane see the truth as a lie because the truth, they got brainwashed as a child under the guise of education, would shatter their world. The sane would have a mental breakdown because if they understood all the sequential education was really just a Trojan horse used to make people mentally slothful and turned their emotions and fear all the way up so they cannot think clearly, they would have to reevaluate everything they have ever known, so because of that they reproach, they criticize the ones who try to tell them that reality because they see that reality as a lie because it is beyond their mental capacity in the brainwashed state of mind to fully grasp. I write books an explain how traditional education, the tree of knowledge, mentally ruins the mind of the person that gets it and they may never be able to escape that mental ruin, and when they hear that they insult me because they do not want that reality to be true. They wish I was on drugs but I am not drunk as they suppose for it is the third hour of the day [Acts 2:15 For these are not drunken, as ye suppose, seeing it is but the third hour of the day.] And the ones who get the traditional education, the scribes, will tell me over and over I speak blaspheme when I speak of the ancient texts [Matthew 9:3 And, behold, certain of the scribes said within themselves, This man blasphemeth.] But I swiftly remind them if they understood one single sentence of the ancient texts, I will remind them. - 12/17/2009 12:52:52 AM

12/18/2009 2:47:03 AM — [1 Timothy 6:10 For the love of money is the root of all evil: which while some coveted after, they have erred from the faith, and pierced themselves through with many sorrows.]
[For the love of money] Love is simply coveting and is not really possible when right brain is unveiled. One cannot maintain a state of love and so one cannot maintain a state of coveting and so one cannot maintain a mental state of greed because right brain ponders to swiftly to the next thought or one way to look at it is the random access aspect of right brain skips around to fast to ever maintain one state of mind such as lust, greed or coveting. A person in the extreme left brain state will perceive love is good but then when what they love is absent they will hate or become depressed but they will say love is good even with the many sorrows that come with this thing they perceive is love. It is not love it is a symptom their mind is unsound and bent to the left and all their emotions are turned up to unsafe level as a result and so it is just suffering.
[love of money is the root of all evil] Before there was money there was bartering.
For example the first people from civilization came to America and meet the Native Americans and they had to barter with them because the Native Americans did not have money so civilization invented money and thus the monetary system. So this comment [money is the root of all evil] is really saying civilization, left brain influenced containers, is the root of all evil. What is civilization based on? Written language and math. One gets the written language and math, their mind is bent to the left and they exhibit mental traits such as coveting, greed, lust, envy

and pride and those traits are all the exact same thing, symptoms of an unsound mind bent to the left.

[Mark 11:15 And they come to Jerusalem: and Jesus went into the temple, and began to cast out them that sold and bought in the temple, and overthrew the tables of the moneychangers, and the seats of them that sold doves;] This comment has nothing to do with the Temples it has to do with civilizations invention, the monetary system and at the end of this comment it is suggesting [and the seats of them that sold doves] and in a monetary system everyone has a product to sell and it is usually their self. A person sells their self for money in order to afford food use to be free. Monetary system is a manmade invention and has nothing to do with natural aspects relative to existence, it is a manmade invention to establish control. If a person does not have money they are not important and if they do have money they are important and that is all an illusion created by a manmade invention called the monetary system. People conditioned in to the extreme left brain state kill their self daily because they do not have money and they stress out because they do not have money and they harm others because they need more money. A person in the neurosis will judge another person based on how much money they have and that is how sick the neurosis makes one and that is how sick civilization is as a whole is a result of pushing this tree of knowledge invention, desired to make one wise. You play by the cults rules, civilization, because if you do not you get thrown into a ditch. People who got the education and didn't apply the remedy will suggest one can always go somewhere else because they are not aware they are simply a cult member and a defender of the cult that mentally hindered their mind as a child under the guise of educating them. This is a symptom of the self esteem issues caused by the neurosis of being in extreme left brain state. Ones in this neurosis cannot even imagine life without the cult, civilization, so they are defenseless as beings. They will complain of the corruption of civilization but they are a part of that corruption and support that corruption and are not even aware they support and defend it. One in the neurosis will argue "If you get an education you will have money." but they are not aware all the money in the universe is not worth losing the complex aspect of their mind, but they will argue it is. So the ones in neurosis are not aware of what they are doing because they only have the slothful aspect of the mind working and the bright aspect of their mind has been reduced to a subconscious aspect. What that means is they are far wiser when they are sleeping at night than when they awake and conscious, they are far wiser when they take lots of drugs to unveil right brain a bit than when they do not take drugs to unveil right brain a bit. They have moments of clarity when they are on mind altering drugs but without the drugs they are essentially mindless specters.

So Jesus was insulting civilization and its ways and he was suggesting the written language caused all of these symptoms, the tree of knowledge and it got some people's attention.

[Mark 11:18 And the scribes and chief priests heard it, and sought how they might destroy him: for they feared him, because all the people was astonished at his doctrine.]

It got the attention of the power structure of civilization, the scribes in power. [the scribes and chief priests heard it] The rulers and the educators who pushed the written education took notice because [all the people was astonished at his doctrine.] The people which are the ruler's slaves were starting to understand what Jesus was saying. One might suggest Jesus was starting to enlighten the slaves to their bondage and the rulers of the cult of civilization did not like that, [the scribes]. Every single person in at least the American government got the education and certainly has not applied the remedy so they are the scribes and the rulers. A chief priest is just a leader or a ruler of the slaves relative to religion or their delusional interpretation of the ancient texts anyway. The rulers will go on into infinity how they only want to help the people, their slaves, but if that was true they would not rape them into mental hell when they are six with the written education. The fruits of the scribe ruler's tree is to make sure everyone gets the written education when they are six. Jesus had faith in what John the Baptist was saying and allowed John to apply his version of the Abraham and Isaac remedy to the education.

[Matthew 3:16 And Jesus, when he was baptized, went up straightway out of the water: and, lo, the heavens were opened unto him, and he saw the Spirit of God descending like a dove, and lighting upon him:]

[the heavens were opened unto him] and his mind opened up and he negated the mental suffering caused by the written education and after civilization, the rulers, Herod cut Johns head off Jesus tried the best he could to continue to "raise the dead" with his version of the remedy until the cult , civilization, butchered him. Because you do not speak English I will explain to you the proper definition of the word scribe. It is a writer. If you can write you are a scribe. The complexity is if you got the written education and then apply the remedy you will not be able to scribe well.

[1 Corinthians 1:20 Where is the wise? where is the scribe? where is the disputer of this world? hath not God made foolish the wisdom of this world?]

World = civilization. This comment is say where are all these wise people your written education is suppose to create civilization, relative to [Genesis 3:6   a tree to be desired to make one wise,] [where is the scribe?] The scribe has their mind bent all the way to the left and the right brain once unveiled makes the scribe look like a fool. Right brain unveiled makes a left brain dominate being look like a fool in contrast. The wisdom of the world, civilization is stupidity because civilization veils the right brain of a child and that child is mentally ruined beyond all definitions of the word ruined. I know that is an absolute fact because I have something you do not have and that is contrast to how I was mentally and how I am after applying the fear not remedy, accidentally.

[Jeremiah 8:8 How do ye say, We are wise, and the law of the LORD is with us? Lo, certainly in vain made he it; the pen of the scribes is in vain.]

How can anyone they understand these ancient texts and believe them when they are scribes and have not applied the remedy? They simply cannot be anything but false in everything they say about the ancient texts if they got the written education and have not applied the fear not remedy.

[the pen of the scribes is in vain.] The ones who get the education might be able to spell words in proper sequence and make it seem like they are wise. The ones who get the education will hold their diploma up and suggest that means they are wise and they are wise as long as ones definition of wise is mentally bent to the left to the extent they are hallucinating, sense time, emotions turned up to maximum, afraid of a bad haircut and words, mentally suffering and only capable of elementary sequential logic. If that is the scribes definition of wisdom then they are in fact infinitely wise. All of civilization, the cult, will say every child needs and education but they do not understand their "brand" of written education veils the right brain and so it is only brainwashing. And so they are only saying "Every child needs to have their complex right brain veiled and put in a mental state of hell and suffering." So all I can suggest is they know not what they do, what they say, what truth is, or what reality is and this is text book definition of a lunatic.

Lunatic : considered thoughtless, ridiculous, or reckless; affected by a psychiatric disorder.

[Matthew 8:19 And a certain scribe came, and said unto him, Master, I will follow thee whithersoever thou goest.]

A certain scribe is simply a person who got the written education. [I will follow thee] simply means this scribe took Jesus' word for it that perhaps his mind was altered by the written education and so he decided to at least attempt to apply the remedy because he had nothing to lose. One is better off with less fear than more fear and the remedy is about losing some of that fear so one cannot go wrong with remedy.

[1 John 4:18 There is no fear in love; but perfect love casteth out fear: because fear hath torment. He that feareth is not made perfect in love.]

If one fears words they are only capable of fear. If one fears the dark they are only capable of fear. [but perfect love casteth out fear] = The remedy takes all the fear away. Neurologically speaking when one is in a position where that hypothalamus gives them the death signal and they relax and do not run in fear, they lose the fear which means the hypothalamus stops sending them all these false alarms of fear and then right brain unveils again. - 4:06:43 AM

5:19:44 AM – Left brain is sequential based and right brain is random access based. So one who gets the written language is conditioned into extreme left brain and see's parts, a left brain trait, and has sequential based thoughts or sequential logic. One who applies the remedy unveils right brain and has random access and sequential based thoughts so their actual thought process is random sequential. Because of this they can understand what the ones conditioned into left brain are saying but the ones conditioned into left brain cannot understand what the ones who have right brain unveiled are saying. A better way to look at it is the ones who apply the remedy are hard to follow in their comments because they are speaking random sequential thoughts and the ones on the left are only able to follow sequential thought comments and that is why this comment was made [Mark 8:21 And he said unto them, How is it that ye do not understand?] So this random sequential thought patter' is normal and means right and left brain are both working at the same time and the sequential thoughts alone means one+s mind is abnormal but in reverse world, random access thoughts are attributed to people who are mentally unsound. Random sequential appears as babbling to ones conditioned to extreme left brain and since nearly everyone is conditioned into extreme left because they all got the education and did not apply the remedy they will all agree that certainly what I write in random sequential only proves I am insane because none of their friends can follow it and neither can they. If a world full of lunatics cannot understand a sane man that certainly must mean the sane man is insane. I do not perceive anyone in civilization is stupid I am just a firm believer in cause and effect relationships. If a person gets their mind bent to the left there is no way they can understand random sequential comments easily and there is also no way a person who applies the remedy and unveils this random sequential thought patterns could speak freely without confusing one who can only understand sequential comments easily, and so that person conditioned into left brain perceives I am on drugs or I need medical help and relative to them that is understandable. The main difference is I understand why they cannot follow my comments from a neurological point of view and all they can come up with is shallow observations because the complexity, a right brain trait, is veiled. A person who dislikes another person usually has an absolute excuse for that dislike. Some dislike people of another race or another country for example. I do not dislike people on that kind of an absolute scale because I am mindful it is not their fault they got this left brain bending "education" as a child. They were a child and they relied on other people to watch out for them and it is unfortunate those people also had their mind bent to the left by the education also. So the paradox is I like civilization because I am mindful they can adjust and apply the remedy and return to sound mind and then be aware of the dangers of written education and I dislike civilization because it will not adjust and understand written education dangerous mental side effects and so it will continue to hinder children's minds juts like its mind was hindered as a child. Civilization could adjust and look into what I suggest and even claim they figured it out their self but the purest form of optimism is ignorance so I digress. - 5:42:23 AM

12:55:02 PM – One important thing to consider is because I write this book in real time I am coming to new understandings as I write and if you are coming to new understandings as you read then the question is : Who is doing the teaching? - 12:56:36 PM

.

12/20/2009 3:23:06 PM — [Luke 23:11 And Herod with his men of war set him at nought, and mocked him, and arrayed him in a gorgeous robe, and sent him again to Pilate.] This comment is relative to this comment [Luke 20:46 Beware of the scribes, which desire to walk in long robes, and love greetings in the markets, and the highest seats in the synagogues, and the chief rooms at feasts;]

[and arrayed him in a gorgeous robe] = [Beware of the scribes, which desire to walk in long robes] This shows that Herod was a scribe or a person who got the written education and did not apply the fear not remedy. This is all relative to rulers and power mongers. [and the highest seats in the synagogues]

[Ecclesiastes 10:19 A feast is made for laughter, and wine maketh merry: but money answereth all things.]. Religious holidays are relative to this comment [Galatians 4:10 Ye observe days, and months, and times, and years.] So this is the initial comment is saying the feasts, holidays are used to make the scribes, ones who did not apply the remedy, happy and merry but in reality the holidays, feasts, are all about money. [but money answereth all things.] This means money is the reason for the holidays not laughter and to be merry.

So this comment is explaining how the power mongers were set on getting rid of Jesus after they got rid of John the Baptist. [Luke 23:12 And the same day Pilate and Herod were made friends together: for before they were at enmity between themselves.] The one thing the power mongers, left brain, will not stand for is losing power, being forced back to 50/50 in harmony with right brain. So although in the texts Pilate appears to be one who is willing to let Jesus go but that is simply not true because he already met with Herod and they decided to get rid of Jesus, so Pilate is simply making it look like he is not guilty or does not have it in for Jesus but in reality this comment [And the same day Pilate and Herod were made friends together:] shows the rulers already decided to do Jesus in. The deeper reality is left brain is going to kill right brain no matter what if it can. So this conspiracy against Jesus, right brain influenced container, by the rulers and the scribes, left brain influenced containers, is contrary to what this suggests [Luke 23:34 Then said Jesus, Father, forgive them; for they know not what they do. And they parted his raiment, and cast lots.] The complexity here is Jesus was referring to the common people who were slaves or servants to the rulers among the scribes. A common day example would be a truant officer who makes sure all the kids go to school to get the education. Another example would be a police officer. Anyone who does harmful things and then suggests it is their job. A police officer may arrest a person for doing drugs for example when in reality that person is addicted to drugs because they are trying to get some relief from the extreme left brain state of mind the written education put them in. So the police officer is a minion of the ruler scribes but also a slave like all the rest because they got the education. So when Jesus was being killed he was killed by the soldiers who were just doing their job but in reality they were doing the bidding of Herod and Pilate, the ruler left brain influenced containers, who had already decided after Jesus was baptized to get rid of Jesus. After the money changer event where Jesus scolded the banks and the economic system based on its usury the ruler scribes knew they had to get rid of Jesus and they did not do it their self they used their minions to get rid of Jesus. Herod set his minions against Jesus and Pilate set his solders against Jesus. So the deeper meaning is the scribes who did not apply the remedy were out to destroy the ones who did apply the remedy. Simply put the doctrine of all these wise beings in all these ancient texts is a simple one yet a powerful one. [Mark

12:38 And he said unto them in his doctrine, Beware of the scribes, which love to go in long clothing, and love salutations in the marketplaces,] The traditional education, written language, is nothing but a mind altering Trojan horse used to make one mentally hindered and thus easy to control. Certainly it is no threat to the Ruler scribes if someone suggests they believe in supernatural. Certainly it is no threat to a Political leader if someone suggests they believe in God. Jesus was not saying he believed in supernatural he was saying [Beware of the scribes] because the scribes will push their script on y"u and it will "inder your mind and you will become the ruler scribes slave, and that is a threat to the (religious) scribe rulers, Herod and to the political scribe ruler, Pilate. The deeper reality is right brain was saying beware of the script, written education, it veils me.

[which love to go in long clothing] = Materialism; because their powerhouse right brain is veiled so all they have is materialism as an outlet.

[and love salutations in the marketplaces] = Money based economic system because once ones right brain is veiled all one has is money to seek rewards and satisfaction from instead of understandings.

Once right brain is veiled one is left with an unviable mind so all they have left is to seek purpose in material things because they are unable seek purpose in cerebral aspects. The only solution the scribes rulers, who do not apply the remedy, have is to kill the ones who apply the remedy because the ones who apply the remedy are so strong in their arguments because "hey have " viable mind.

[Luke 4:32 And they were astonished at his doctrine: for his word was with power.]

(They) the ruler scribes were astonished Jesus was going to wake up all their slaves because Jesus had a very convincing argument using his words. And the doctrine was [Mark 12:38 And he said unto them in his doctrine, Beware of the scribes,] Perhaps you should go ask your cult leader if that is truth, perhaps. So the minions of the scribes were killing all these wise beings who were only trying to make the minions aware they had been put to sleep using written language, script, as the opiate and because the minions were so mentally hindered, they were not even aware they were killing the good guys and protecting the taskmaster, and relative to what was done to you mentally as a child as a result of all that left brain sequential traditional education, it would be a factual miracle, if you understood that. - 4:25:40 PM

Syrup on your hands - http://www.youtube.com/watch?v=PDAgNSmAKiE

Trying to escape your custody battle
Teens survive without a saddle
Everyone defends what they cannot defend
Everyone wins what they cannot win
The local crowds always get it
The fringe finds a way to regain thought insane
They seem venerated
The ice melts but then it flows

They are not very heroic
Their feet above the ground but no one knows it
That's the proof of the magic of the tragic
The magic is through tragic
The ice melts but then it flows
They're recognized but seldom realized
Devine interceding their light is somewhat fleeting
It's not tangible with time

Exploitated with their hot cakes; syrup on your hands
Exonerated with their miss takes, white noise
Their leaders are false truth; syrup on your hands
Their goodness is the lie tooth; white noise ha
Their wisdom is the greatest fake
Their offspring are for your sake; white noise ha
Their offspring will not try to lie; mystery in the brand
White noise ah
Their offspring with puzzle you dry
Mystery in the brand
Mystery in the brand
Don't think to hard you will only get lost
Mystery in the brand
Don't pay too much you'll only get bossed; syrup on your hands

8:48:40 PM – The brain is essentially the nervous system in vertebrates so once the mind is bent to the left as a result of written education the person becomes a nervous wreck. For example when a person gets nervous in this extreme left brain state they have to urinate and that is abnormal and a symptom they are a nervous wreck. Some in this extreme left brain state get nervous and overeat. Some get nervous and under eat. Some get nervous and take drugs and some harm others or their self. So the mind is relative to the brain and once the mind is bent to the left as a result of the written language "education" everything goes haywire. Civilization as we know it is nothing but a symptom of as species that knowingly or unknowingly altered its mind by improperly learning a perception altering invention called written language. Civilization is simply the fruit of a species that is a nervous wreck. Some of this species will actually harm each other or their self because of the sounds of words. One cannot get any more insane than that, but perhaps one can get less insane than that. So fear is nothing but a symptom one is a nervous wreck because their perceptions has been altered as a result of the many years of left brain "education." Since fear is the main symptom fear not is the main remedy. Mediation for example is one way for a being in this nervous wreck state to try and relax. Many drugs also makes the person relax and this means they do drugs just to escape this nervous wreck state of mind the traditional education put them in. All of the rules spoken and unspoken in fact make's the person in the extreme left brain state more nervous. I was watching a show were a person was caught by the police with marijuana and he had a nervous breakdown. He was crying out to god to save him from being caught by the police for having the drugs. He mentioned his parents would kill him and so it was best if the police just killed him. The final blame falls on the heads of the ruling class who push this traditional education on people. If said ruling class of the scribes is not aware of traditional education dangers then they should not be leaders, and if they are aware of traditional education dangers and do not alter their "education" teachings then they should be infinitely nervous at this stage of my accident. I could use a little fear right about now but it does not seem to be panning out. I keep forgetting I have freedom of speech and if anyone infringes on that I have the right to abolish them.[That whenever any Form of Government becomes destructive of these ends, it is the [Right] of the People to alter or to abolish it], and to institute new Government,]. I'm a people. Goliaths forehead looks infinitely large at this point since the accident but I doubt it.- 9:06:22 PM

11:05:28 PM – I posted this on a neurology forum.
Traditional Education is sequential based.
A six year old child is encouraged to memorize the ABC's.
The ABC's are in sequential order.
Later that young child is given spelling tests graded on that child's ability to arrange letters in sequential order.
If the child spells a word in proper sequential order they are rewarded with a good grade and if not they are punished with a poor grade.
Neurologically what this in fact does is conditions a young child's mind to embrace left brain, it is sequential based and in turn it discourages right brain, it is random access based.
Math is the same situation. Numbers are all in sequential order. Addition and subtraction are simply encouraging a person's ability to sequence.
After even five or six years of this education the minds bents to the left.
This bending causes in fact alters the child perception this is because it affect the cerebral cortex, the amygdala and hypothalamus. Some children become afraid, embarrassed, ashamed and start exhibiting any number of psychological emotional problems.
For example when a child is very young they show few inhibitions and may even say things in public that embarrass their parents but this is because right brain is contrary to left brain and left brain loves rules and so right brain has no concept of rules. Rules hinder right brains ability to detect patterns and also hinders right brain complexity.
The only way to avoid this mental left brain bending is for the child to only get oral education until their minds develops fully but this is certainly not the case. At the age of even 4 in some cases the child's mind has been bent so far to teh left they start showing symptoms. Suicides start at about the age of 14 in children. Children start experimenting with drugs. This age is in fact the point at which that child has gone clinically insane from having their mind bent so far to the left from years of traditional written sequential education.

One very obvious symptom of this education induced neurosis is sense of time. The reason a person sense of time is so strong is because right brain ambiguity is essentially veiled. When right brain is working in harmony with left brain the ambiguity does not allow a person to sense time because when a person try's to determine how much time has passed the right brain ambiguity tells them much time has passed and no time has passed , and that is the minds final answer so one cannot tell how much time has passed. This is also relative to the paradox that is a trait of right brain.

When a person fears a word for example a cuss word it is a symptom their mind has bent so far to the left as a result of traditional education the hypothalamus is sending them false signal of fear. Many fear words will harm them but it is impossible a sound can harm anyone so that person is in fact hallucinating because their hypothalamus is not working properly in the left bent state of mind. So the only remedy to this neurosis is to first off start saying perhaps often in every sentence one speaks because perhaps is ambiguity and this favors right brain. The absolute remedy is to reach a situation where one can get the hypothalamus to give them a false signal of death. For example a person may watch a scary movie then turn off the lights and when that hypothalamus gives them the "death", fight or flight a spook is coming to get you, signal that person ignores it or does not rush to turn the lights and this shocks the hypothalamus back into working order and unveils right brain. After this remedy is applied it may take a month for right brain to be restored or unveiled.

Right brain is so fast and ponders so fast, it is known as subconscious, which proves it is veiled, many emotional problems are not possible. Depression, embarrassment and many other emotional problems cannot be maintained for more than a moment because right brain ponder so fast from thought to thought, so sadness cannot be maintained after this "remedy" is applied.

The brain is the nervous system so once the mind is bent far to the left by traditional education one is essentially becomes a nervous wreck not to mention one is stuck with sequential thoughts and is susceptible to fear of words, shadows, music and nudity so they are a text books example of a hallucinating neurotic. Freud suggest "Neurosis is the inability to tolerate ambiguity." Ambiguity is a right brain trait. So if perhaps of one has trouble saying perhaps at the begging and ending of every sentence even around friends and peers then perhaps they are neurotic , perhaps. END - 11:06:07 PM

12/21/2009 5:31:31 AM — [Acts 8:9 But there was a certain man, called Simon, which beforetime in the same city used sorcery, and bewitched the people of Samaria, giving out that himself was some great one:
Acts 8:10 To whom they all gave heed, from the least to the greatest, saying, This man is the great power of God.]

Sorcery is the supposed use of magic. An example of this is a person who says they will pray to God to save you. An example of this is a person who suggests they will pray to God to cure you of a disease. An example of this is a person who suggests supernatural powers or knowledge of supernatural powers. An example is a person who brings a little old lady in a wheel chair up on stage and prays to their supernatural and makes everyone believe they healed that lady by praying to supernatural and then asks for a love offering of money. A sorcerer bewitches people out of their money using untruth and deceit; essentially they are bold faced liars in the name of money.

[To whom they all gave heed] Means the ones conditioned into the extreme left brain state all idolize that person and give that person money and babble on about how much God works through him in his great feats of healing old lady's in wheel chairs so everyone will give him money.

[from the least to the greatest, saying, This man is the great power of God.] A sorcerer has the power of fraud not God. I am mindful there are beings who are suffering enough from having their mind bent all the way to the left from traditional education who only want to escape that mental suffering caused by a manmade invention taught by beings who have no mental function to understand they are literally killing beings as a direct result of teaching said traditional education improperly. There is only one thing going through a being minds in this extreme left brain state just before they kill their self as a result of the many years of mental suffering. They are thinking, "I just want to escape this mental suffering state of mind." and they are willing to kill their self to escape. If any of these sorcerers could detect supernatural I will remind them.

At this very moment these sorcerers are preparing to celebrate, one of their feasts and holidays, the fact they killed the truth. The sorcerer scribes will encourage everyone to buy gifts for each other to celebrate the fact they killed the truth. They will kill the truth in one second and then suggest they can detect supernatural. I see them with their robes lined in gold and then they will explain how they have a direct line to God. These experts on supernatural are simply in the den of the whore and the golden calf and I assure you I spit in their face openly. If they understood one single sentence in the ancient texts I will remind them.

[Acts 13:6 And when they had gone through the isle unto Paphos, they found a certain sorcerer, a false prophet, a Jew, whose name was Barjesus:]

[Acts 13:7 Which was with the deputy of the country, Sergius Paulus, a prudent man; who called for Barnabas and Saul, and desired to hear the word of God.]

[Acts 13:8 But Elymas the sorcerer (for so is his name by interpretation) withstood them, seeking to turn away the deputy from the faith.]

[Acts 13:9 Then Saul, (who also is called Paul,) filled with the Holy Ghost, set his eyes on him,]

[Acts 13:10 And said, O full of all subtilty and all mischief, thou child of the devil, thou enemy of all righteousness, wilt thou not cease to pervert the right ways of the Lord?]

First off the initial spirit I get from this section is humor. Paul is running around calling the scribes who did not apply the fear not remedy the devil. [thou child of the devil]

Now the complexity of this is perhaps there was not a word called "full blown neurosis brainwashed sequential based abomination as a result of civilization mentally raping you into mental hell with their written language desired to make one wise, invention".

[they found a certain sorcerer, a false prophet, a Jew,] This comment has created lots of hate towards the Jews and this is because the ones who see things as parts believe the words or assume the words suggest absolutes. Relative to this time period a Jew was simply a person who got the written education and then applied the fear not remedy to negate the unwanted mental side effects of the written language, the extreme left brain mindset. That is what a Jew is, so Paul is in fact saying this Jew is a false Jew, false prophet, a scribe. A person cannot get years of written education and then assume they are a Jew, Christian, Muslim, Buddhist or Philosopher just because they can say those words. Just because someone says they are a Jew or some other religion means nothing if one has not applied the fear not, deny ones self, submit to perceived death, go sit in a cemetery until you feel better, remedy. So Paul was in fact making a comment that John repeated in Revelations [Revelation 3:9 Behold, I will make them of the synagogue of Satan, which say they are Jews, and are not, but do lie; behold, I will make them to come and worship before thy feet, and to know that I have loved thee.]
[[they found a certain sorcerer, a false prophet, a Jew,] = [which say they are Jews, and are not, but do lie; behold]
One can interchange the word Jew for Christian, Muslim, Buddhist or Philosopher. Think about a Christian "preacher" and you see him on television and he has a gold Rolex and fine linen and he is suggesting you send him money so he can heal an old lady in a wheel chair so you will send him even more money. That being is a false Prophet because if that being in fact applied the fear not, deny one's self remedy he would be fully aware of the extent of suffering the traditional education causes and he would discover suggesting traditional education in fact mentally hinders a person into mental hell, would reduce his flock to just him and he would realize he is one against six billion and would be quite humbled. The deeper reality is just convincing a person firstly the traditional education has veiled their right brain is difficult enough, then to convince them they have to apply the fear not remedy, that's a lifelong profession alone, so a person is simply unable to bring money into it because money serves no purpose. The odds of convincing someone to apply the remedy the full measure, defeat their fear of death is in the realm of impossible so one does not want to allow anything to hinder their chances. Deeper still a person was a child when the left brain bending education was pushed on them so it is not their fault, they were a trusting child and they were taken advantage of so there is no need to charge because they are an innocent victim of the cult, civilization, the left brain influenced containers. Of course right brain hates rules so there is nothing set in stone about money, once one applies the remedy, they make their own determinations I just happen to kill myself because I had no money so I have an aversion to it, and that is my flaw.

115

[they found a certain sorcerer, a false prophet,] So this comment is suggesting a person who suggests they have magical powers and a person who says they have a direct line to God or can do things because of supernatural is a sorcerer and a false prophet because the tree of knowledge is a manmade invention and the remedy is a mental process based in reality not supernatural. Perhaps you do understand written language was invented by man and so its mental side effects are the result of mankind assuming he could invent something that has no bad side effects which is impossible. Even the internet appeared like a great invention until it put all the news papers out of business and a host of other professions and businesses and now we are staring to understand we keep inventing things that have side effects we did not perceive happening but then it is too late to adjust and correct it. This is exactly what written education has done. It's a great inventions and took vast intelligence to invent and no question about that but it has some mental side effects that are equally devastating if it is not taught properly. This has nothing to do with supernatural at all. Perhaps the complexity is ones who see parts see natural things and supernatural things as separate. One who only see's holistically would not see any difference in the two. Perhaps I do not detect supernatural because I am and that is logical. I am in a bubble and so I see what I am doing as natural but it is not natural at all. I am mindful to be open minded since I am rather blinded by the light so to speak, psychologically speaking, what have you. Granted I fell of the thought train.

[Which was with the deputy of the country] Sergius Paulus was a person in a position of power relative to civilization. What one will perhaps never find in civilization is a person without traditional education in a position of power. A ruler would not run around boasting they should be elected because they have no traditional education and this is symptom of the reverse thing. Civilization has made up its mind a long time ago anyone who does not get the written education cannot possibly be wise and that is relative to the comment in Genisis [Genesis 3:6 And when the woman saw that the tree was good for food, ., and a tree to be desired to make one wise]

Traditional education is desired to make one wise but in reality it veils the right brain so it makes one mentally hindered or retarded so one has to go through this remedy process just to get back to square one and the reality is they may never be able to do that because it is quite a task to accomplish mentally. So there are all these genius beings on the planet who believe they are not wise because they did not get enough traditional education but in reality because they did not get as much traditional education as some of these "rulers" they are in a better position mentally than the rulers mentally. The ones who did not get lots of education are the poor in spirit and are in a better mental position than the ones who got lots of traditional education. So in reality one should be judged by how little traditional education they received not how much they received and this again is the reverse thing. Civilization should be down in the Amazon begging those natives to teach them things because those natives in the Amazon are perhaps the only handful of human beings on this planet that are still mentally sound and mentally untarnished by this written education neurosis but in fact they want nothing to do with civilization. Those natives are wise enough to stay away from neurotic hallucinating mental abominations, so to speak.

[Sergius Paulus, a prudent man; who called for Barnabas and Saul, and desired to hear the word of God.] So this prudent ruler was at least curious to hear the argument of Baranabas and Saul, his cup was not full, so to speak. This is very important after one applies to remedy to keep in mind. One will never be able to tell who the curious ones are. One always gets it no matter what group they are in. The rule of thumb is ones lower on the ladder relative to civilization are a bit more open minded but there is potential in any crowd. Human beings are curious by nature but sometimes shattering their illusions does not go over well. Some resist the truth about traditional education because it is very deep. Speaking about ghosts and aliens is nothing in contrast to explaining to a person who has not applied the remedy traditional education is devastating on the mind if not taught properly. It seems strange because one would think a person would laugh at ghosts and aliens and listen carefully about the bad side effects of an actual real thing, traditional education, but it is just the reverse.

[But Elymas the sorcerer (for so is his name by interpretation) withstood them, seeking to turn away the deputy from the faith.] This comment alone is why some who try to "wake others" perceive it is best to get a person alone to explain this written education truth to. After you apply the remedy you may find yourself in a situation where you are explaining your "strategic words" in a crowd , chat room or in person and some will be curious. Your intuition will tell you that you are reaching one and then another one will say "What drugs are you on?" and then that curious one will also become not so curious. This is simply because some are in such deep neurosis and suffering they want others to stay in that misery also. You will discover you can have a perfect explanation and cover every detail and some will start to "see the light" and then a person will say "You can't even spell well so nothing you say can be true." and that will destroy all your efforts. This should be looked at as an emotional conditioning opportunity. The sane will hear complexity and truth for an hour and then in one witty comment they will negate it all. [seeking to turn away the deputy from the faith.] and that is what this comment is explaining.

Some are in such deep mental suffering because their mind is bent so far to the left they desire no one should ever escape the suffering so they go out of their way to make sure no one gets out of the suffering and what is complex is they perceive they are wise when in reality they have no idea what they are saying or doing. This may appear like some sort of possession but in reality they are under the influence of left brain only and the wise right brain aspect is veiled so they perceive they are capable of complex thoughts and intuition to detect the truth but they are not at all capable of those things. They are trapped in their bubble of perception and their right brain is veiled so what they perceive is wisdom is really simpleminded sequential thoughts and intellect, left brain traits, and are only capable of moments of complexity, intuition and pattern detection on a scale of a few times in their life when they should have these traits at all times.

[Acts 13:9 Then Saul, (who also is called Paul,) filled with the Holy Ghost, set his eyes on him,]
[Acts 13:10 And said, O full of all subtilty and all mischief, thou child of the devil, thou enemy of all righteousness, wilt thou not cease to pervert the right ways of the Lord?]

I am pleased with the humor in this because I can relate to this very well. This psychologically is complex because Paul knew exactly what Elymas was doing but Elymas perceived he was doing a righteous thing steering Sergius Paulus away from listening to Paul and Barnabas. I can go into a chat room and starts explaining the spirit of what I explain in these poorly disguised thick pamphlet diaries and some people well start to understand and then some OP or a person in power in the chat room will say "Shut up you are a false teacher." and then I explode. Not in the way you may perceive explode but it is more like anger waxing as Moses experienced. It's a frustration and a sense of impossibility. This in fact is good because right brain adapts and gets better as a result of this. I look back and ponder what makes me angry and then I ponder it and within a moment I fall back into neutral state of mind. After so many times being called a liar and on drugs and stupid and false, one has a tendency to give up but right brain looks at it as a chance to get better at explaining the situation and one might perceive eventually one will get so good they will explain it flawlessly but that is underestimating how devastating the left brain neurosis is. As a whole this written education has permanently mentally doomed the species. A deeper reality is left brain simply refuses to take its proper seat behind right brain. Because of that one has to use that reality as a strength or they will destroy their self by giving up. This written education neurosis goes back over 5000 years so any being who perceives it can just be defeated is not thinking clearly. The bottom line equation is simply this.

X = ones who are convinced to apply the remedy yearly
Y = Children civilization conditions into the neurosis state of mind with written education yearly.

X is always less than Y.

It is exactly like bailing out a boat with a teaspoon while gallons of water pour into the boat in the same period of time one bails one teaspoon of water out of the boat. Civilization, the "rulers" in civilization are never going to submit written education has major mental side effect because if they did they would hang their self. Civilization does not have the ability to compensate people for the mental damage they have done to them with written education being taught improperly so civilization, the rulers, are never ever going to even look into the potential unwanted mental side effects of written education because if the media ever caught wind civilization, the rulers, were looking into the potential mental side effects of all that sequential education on the mind, society as a whole would erupt in all out revolution against the rulers of civilization. Civilization is not going to come out and say "By the way all that left brain education we forced on you by law made you a mentally hindered retard and you may not be able to undo the damage, our bad."

The good news is it is not illegal to say "perhaps" at the beginning and ending of every sentence you speak so that is a form of favoring right brain. It is not illegal to listen to music you dislike. This will assist you in prepping your mind to apply the main remedy, which is to get that hypothalamus to send you the death signal and then you ignore that signal.

[[Acts 13:10 And said, O full of all subtilty and all mischief, thou child of the devil, thou enemy of all righteousness, wilt thou not cease to pervert the right ways of the Lord?]

So here is where Paul was scolding Elymas for steering the "ruler" Sergius Paulus from listening to Paul's explanation about the mental side effects of written language, the tree of knowledge. Paul understood if he could reach a ruler in civilization and convince that ruler about the side effects of written language on the mind if not taught properly he would have won. If I could convince the board of education I win. If I can convince a majority of psychologists I win. But the ultimate reality of that is compensation to the victims. What about a person who is spent their entire life addicted to drugs just so they could escape the mental suffering the written education put them in. What about a rapist in prison who is only a rapist because they were coveting, and that is because their right brain was veiled as a child because of the education. What about a mother whose child killed their self because they were cyber bullied and could not handle the depression caused by that because that child was conditioned into extreme left brain as a result of the education. The mental suffering caused by this traditional education invention not being taught properly is so vast that the species would perhaps be unable to face the reality of such extreme suffering. Every single person who got this education and then applies the remedy and discovers what they were robbed of, their right brain, would perhaps want heads on stakes. I am mindful the mind itself is trying to answer one question after the remedy is applied, "What did I do to you that you would do this to me as a child." One can never escape that question after they apply the remedy to the full measure, and so that is their motivation to tell others. Granted I fell off the tracks. - 8:20:57 AM

3:49:29 PM – This is the final comment of the above [thou enemy of all righteousness, wilt thou not cease to pervert the right ways of the Lord?]

[Righteousness], [right ways of the Lord.] = right brain ways = random access, complexity, paradox etc.

This rhetorical question is a repeat of this rhetorical question [Psalms 74:10 O God, how long shall the adversary reproach? shall the enemy blaspheme thy name for ever?]

When all indications point to defeat lean into it.- 6:24:38 PM

Right brain does not like rules. It is contrary to left brain on one hand so that is logical right brain would not like rules because left brain likes rules and rules create a sense of order relative to left brain. So then a control system is based on rules so right brain would get in the way of any control system. If a person says do not say that word or you are bad then that is a subtle form of control. It is essentially an absolute (if then) statement. (If) anyone says this word (then) they are bad. So(if) a person says that word (then) they are deemed bad and they gain a reputation for not following the rules. So now that (if then) statement turns into an (if then else) statement,(If) a person says that word (then) they are bad (else) they follow rules. So now that rule is simply a scare tactic. These scare tactics only work on people who have an ego or pride, and ego and pride are symptoms of being conditioned into the extreme left brain by traditional education. One can alter everything they do in life if they try to preserve their pride and ego. Perhaps a better way to look at these pride and ego aspects is being self conscious. For example some people are self conscious about their weight so they are self conscious about their body and that leads to self esteem issues and that is not because that person is naturally self conscious it is because that persons mind has been bent to the left. A native tribe has women that do not wear tops so they are not self conscious but if a person who gets the education goes there, that person will be self conscious that the women do not wear tops. A person who is self conscious is really ashamed.
[Genesis 2:25 And they were both naked, the man and his wife, and were not ashamed.]
This comment is pre tree of knowledge, written education. Being ashamed of your body or your thought's is abnormal because one can never escape those things. If one is ashamed of their body or their thoughts then they have huge self esteem issues and those self esteem issues lead to emotional problems and emotional problems lead to a large branch of problems. Words are a symptom of thoughts so one should never be ashamed of their words. The mind has infinite thoughts but there are not infinite words so the thoughts cannot be fully described verbally so sometimes different thoughts are given the same word. One in the extreme left brain state believes certain words are bad words so they do not use them in say a public forum because they assume they will be called stupid or bad. A child in school is fully aware if they "cuss" in class they will perhaps get a paddling and then suspended and then punished by their parents, so that child is controlled and also that child's mind is controlled by threat of punishment, so that is simply a fear tactic used on a small child. A small child may hear a cuss word and then repeat that cuss word but not perceive it is a bad word until they are punished for saying that word verbally or physically so they are conditioned to fear words by the adults. The adults are quite certain if they say a cuss word it means they are bad or stupid or uneducated but they simply cannot explain exactly why they would be those things if they say a cuss word. All of these subtle control mechanisms are all based on fear tactics and ironically the traditional education makes one susceptible to all sorts of fear. After even five years of education some children do

not even speak because they are so embarrassed and ashamed to speak. I recall I would think about what would be the perfect thing to say and I always determined it was not the perfect thing to say so I would not speak. I was so scared of words I was reduced to silence. It is unhealthy to not say what's on your mind no matter where it is, and it is even more unhealthy to censor your words because one is afraid of what may happen. One has to come up with words, then they have to measure who is in the room before they can give their self permission to say those words. One has to first gauge how the crowd will react so to speak before they will give their self permission to speak and that hesitation is a symptom of fear. A person is always thinking in their mind "If I say these words what will be the consequences." The reality is there are no consequences for saying words unless one is surrounded by beings in deep neurosis who fear words and thus sounds. Cussing when one slams their hand in a door for example reduces the pain and the reason the pain is reduced is because when one breaks these perceived cuss word rules they favor right brain and for that moment right brain ambiguity kicks in and they are unable to tell how bad the pain is. After a person breaks a rule, any rule, they feel a rush and that is right brain and they are favoring right brain and it dislikes rules and so breaking rules favors right brain for a moment. Once one applies the remedy they will start to lose their ability to see rules. This does not suggest they will go harm people or break the law this only suggests right brain cannot have complexity and pattern detection and rules also. Rules are contrary to paradox. A paradox is two contradictions that make up a truth but rules are absolute, so rules do not allow contradictions. A law is a rule so a law is contrary to right brain. The education system is full of rules and not rules as in laws, just rules. Etiquette is interesting because it is a code and expectations according to norms within society or authority. So etiquette is nothing but a well disguised fear tactic. Relative to the etiquette of civilization the native women who do not wear tops are evil, dumb, stupid or uneducated but that is not possible. So there is a certain sense that people have to subscribe to these rules based on the norms of society or they are bad people, and that is what a fear tactic is. A person with fear does not want it to get around they are bad based on the fact they broke etiquette created by some group of people who perceive there is etiquette. There is no etiquette, only people who suggest there is and fools who believe them. Freedom removes rules and so as tyranny increases rules increase. No one knows how many unspoken rules there are in civilization and that means civilization essentially favors left brain. All one ever has to do is say it is proper etiquette to do this certain thing and left brain influenced containers will line up for miles do that thing. There are thousands of rules relative to fashion, what to wear and what not to wear and one can be certain they will be shunned and embarrassed if they break any of those rules. When right brain is unveiled it cannot be embarrassed or ashamed because it does not detect any rules. If a person believes a word can be bad they are nothing but a slave their fear of that word and so they are a slave to their own perceptions. If one is in deep space and they say all the cuss words in the universe absolutely nothing will happen and the reality is earth is in deep space. A parent did not come up with the etiquette that cuss words are bad they were told cuss words are bad so they punish their child for saying cuss words because they believed the person who told them cuss words are certainly evil or bad or a symptom of evil or bad. Civilization is against right brain because civilization is based on conformity and right brain is based on non conformity. "My way or the highway" is nothing but a cheap scare tactic to get someone to do what they want you to do, so it is the trick of a tyrant. "Give me liberty or give me death" is the answer to "My way or the highway." When one of these control freaks in civilization proves to me they are god I will consider ignoring fewer of their rules than I ignore now. The last I checked the etiquette of civilization suggested I get my mind bent to the left as a child to the point it turned all my emotions up and it almost killed me, so I will remind civilization, if I ever listen to your rules, laws or opinions again ever into infinity, you can assume I have gone insane.

I am mindful when I start a thought line I usually end up with an anger comment. I have no emotional capacity so I try to have emotions with words because I am not use to being in neutral. It is as if I am trying to emulate how I use to be and I cannot do that so I do the next best thing and that is use anger words but they do not work. I no longer feel anything whether I say a cuss word or the word love or happy so the words do not work anymore in relation to they do not excite my emotions because right brain ponders so fast emotions are strictly a symptom of a slothful left brain thought processing. Look how angry these words Paul used

[Acts 13:10 And said, O full of all subtilty and all mischief, thou child of the devil, thou enemy of all righteousness,..]

Devil certainly must have been a cuss word back then as well as "full of subtilty and all mischief." Subtilty denotes light or thin as in mentally shallow. So Paul is saying you are shallow and just a joker or a prankster which means Paul is trying to be serious and this being he is talking to thinks it is all a joke or is unable to grasp what he is saying. What is even deeper about all of this is every time Paul says someone is a devil or insults them it goes against the etiquette of the norms of civilization so it breaks rules so Paul encourages right brain even more. So Paul is using these people as fear conditioning tools in order to favor right brain more. Once you apply the remedy if you go around fearing to speak your mind you slowly start to favor left brain again because left brain is all about rules and regulations. The truth is you may never convince anyone to apply this remedy and you may never make any progress in convincing society of the mental dangers of traditional education but you do have the freedom to better yourself.

[Matthew 7:5 Thou hypocrite, first cast out the beam out of thine own eye; and then shalt thou see clearly to cast out the mote out of thy brother's eye.]

The extreme fear caused by the conditioning must be removed in order to think clearly. The trick is one cannot tell how much fear there is to remove. So Paul was speaking to people in high ranking in society, and insulting them because he was afraid to do that, so in doing that he lost a little more fear.

[first cast out the beam out of thine own eye; and then shalt thou see clearly]

This is a repeat of Tho I walk through the valley of the shadow of death I fear no evil and a repeat of those who lose their life will preserve it and also a repeat of fear not which Abraham suggested and submit, and also deny one's self. If one is afraid to say something and they say it they deny their self. Every time one denies what that extreme left brain suggests they favor right brain and slowly silence the left brain until they reach a point of 50/50 mental harmony. Because of the nature of the neurosis caused by the traditional education one in fact has to be a concentration master [and then shalt thou see clearly to cast out the mote out of thy brother's eye.] One will be able to see clearly, which is think clearly, then they might be able to assist the ones in deep neurosis. The better one gets at concentration and thus cerebral thought the less the material world matters. It is not material things are bad it is simply in the cerebral world material things tend to take a back seat. One does not have to give away their material things to apply this remedy. You work hard enough for the material things so try to look at it as the material things you have will not be so important after you apply the remedy relative to your perception of them. Right brain ambiguity is going to always tell a person that perhaps money is not worth harming someone over and so that doubt is going to not allow a person or perceive great value in material things. The ambiguity in right brain means one is not a good judge on many things, like sense of time, sense of hunger, sense of pain. One is always left with the final answer being a paradox. Maybe you are hungry and maybe you are not and that final answer is neutral. Somewhere in that neutral you end up eating but then your mind says maybe you are full or maybe you are not full and that final answer is neutral. I speak with people who have not applied the remedy and I see them and sense them as fantastic but I still try to suggest words to convince them to apply the remedy. So that is a paradox, they are perfect but I try to suggest they change. I want them to apply the remedy but I am not allowed to force them to apply the remedy. I want to make a convincing argument but I am not allowed to force them so I come across as funny but I am not funny and this is not a game and I mean business but the paradox is real and the ambiguity is real so the ones who are trying to "wake up" others are trapped by their perception. I am mindful this is why this neurosis has gone on so long in our species and is why it perhaps can never be controlled. Whatever you think about other predications relative to mankind Adam puts them all to shame because he knew 5000 years ago exactly what this tree of knowledge would all lead to :

[Genesis 2:17 But of the tree of the knowledge of good and evil, thou shalt not eat of it: for in the day that thou eatest thereof thou shalt surely die.]

Civilization will suggest recorded history started 2000 years ago but in reality recorded history started the minute this written language was invented perhaps 5400 years ago and that is because it ushered in this strong sense of time one has in the extreme left brain state caused by learning written education. There is a reason Mohammed spoke about Adam in the Quran. Adam was perhaps the first human being relative to the world who woke up from the neurosis caused by written language and figured everything out relative to what its eventuality would lead to relative to mankind. The ones who unveil right brain are hesitant and have lots of ambiguity and are not controlling, and the ones in the neurosis are control freaks and will kill children to get a little more control so this is why this whole situation is unsolvable. What is mysterious is the remedy is quite easy to apply but if a person does not believe they need to apply it after 12 years of left brain education then they will never apply it. This unsolvable reality is kind of a buffer because one who has applied the remedy has to face this impossibility so they do not go mad. One does not become stressed over impossibility. Failing at impossibility is less stressful than failing at possibility. - 8:24:55 PM

12/22/2009 8:16:03 AM – The pattern detection of right brain is so powerful it can sort through ideas and piece them all together and so it gives the impression of intelligence but in reality it is more relative to pattern detection and then making those patterns convince others of intelligence. There is a movie called Dances with Wolves. There are patterns I detect but it does not means what I suggest it true relative to this movie it is simply right brain detects patterns and then explains those patterns in a convincing way.

At the start of the movie the main character gets his foot injured and then the Doctor says he has to take the foot off. This is a stress or panic that is created in the main character. This would be like a person who loses their job, loss. So the main character finds out his foot is coming off, loss, and so he is stressed. The next moment he decides since his foot is coming off there is no point in going on with life. This is similar to a person who becomes depressed for one reason or another. The main character decides to ride out on the battle field. This scene is in the civil war and he is on the north side and fighting against the south. The main character jumps on a horse and rides out on the battle field towards the south and then the General on the north says "Looks like a suicide." So the main character rides across the lines of the south and the southern troops all fire at him. This is in fact a legit suicide attempt. The main character is riding across the line thinking the south will shoot him but they miss and so he reaches the end of the line and turns around and this time he holds his hands up in the air and rides across the southern lines again as the south shoot at him. This is essentially what the remedy is. The main character's mind does not know if he will be shot or not so the main character is letting go or going through the valley of the shadow of death and fearing not. So the main character perceives he is attempting suicide but the fate in this situation is all the southern guys miss him when they shoot at him.

Jesus said let a man deny himself or if one wants to follow me they have to deny their self and that means they have to deny that left brain dominate state of mind caused by traditional education.

[Ecclesiastes 4:5 The fool foldeth his hands together, and eateth his own flesh.]

This comment is suggesting one denies their self, the left brain extreme self. I was very foolish to take pills to kill myself and then I was very foolish to not call for help when my hypothalamus said "You will die if you do not call for help." Nothing about that situation appeared wise or reasonable yet in reality is was very reasonable and very wise. So this main character rode his horse in front of the southern lines and that was very foolish appearing. Then he not only rode once but he rode twice against the southern lines and that was even more foolish. So relative to the Northern general who said "Looks like a suicide" what the main character was doing was foolish but relative to reality the main character was

124

denying himself so it was wise because he was unknowingly escaping the left brain state which caused him to perceive because his foot was going to be cut off he had no reason to live anymore. Relative to Dante the main character was in the treason circle of hell, the 9th circle. Suicide is treason against one's self and Jesus said deny one's self and that is mental suicide.

[Matthew 5:3   ¶Blessed are the poor in spirit: for theirs is the kingdom of heaven.

Matthew 5:4 Blessed are they that mourn: for they shall be comforted.

Matthew 5:5 Blessed are the meek: for they shall inherit the earth.

Matthew 5:6 Blessed are they which do hunger and thirst after righteousness: for they shall be filled.]

[poor in spirit] = [they that mourn] = [the meek] = [they which do hunger and thirst after righteousness] = the depressed = the suicidal = ones in the 9th circle of hell, treason

A person who is depressed in spirit is sad or they are mentally sad and that is a symptom of the end result of being in the extreme left brain state. A suicidal person mentally is mourning or their mind cannot take this mental suffering any longer caused by being in the left brain state, so they are meek because they perceive they are not even important enough to remain alive and so subconsciously they are seeking the kingdom which means they are seeking to wake up and unveil right brain. They hunger to escape this extreme left brain state the traditional education has put them in but many do not make it because this is not an absolute thing, this waking up, and many who reach the 9th circle of hell, treason usually end up killing their self or getting so many drugs thrown at them they climb back into the 8th or 7th circle of hell. When a person is born right brain is unveiled but it is not fully developed, the mind. So then right brain is veiled by traditional education and right brain is going to do anything I can to get unveiled because that is the trend. Another way to look at it is right brain should not be veiled on a scale of absolute normalcy so right brain will do things to become unveiled that appear strange to an observer. This is an indication how difficult it is to unveil right brain without using any right brain favoring techniques. Right brain understands what it has to do to get out but when it is veiled it has been reduced to a subconscious level and these subconscious signals from right brain come out in a person on a conscious level in strange ways. Simply put right brain will kill the being to get out of its veiled state because right brain is either going to get out or it prefers to be dead. Right brain is so powerful even from a veiled subconscious state it controls that persons thoughts. This main character perceived he was committing suicide or attempting it but in reality right brain was trying to break free but it did not seem like that to observers. This is relative to what an observer see's is not always what is really happening. Jesus said one has to deny their self to follow him and that is not reasonable relative to some but it is very reasonable considering the deny one's self is denying that extreme left brain state of mind caused by traditional education. Some people will suggest you should love yourself but Jesus aid you should deny yourself, relative to self being the state of mind one is in after the traditional education.

This comment appears to be unreasonable.

[Luke 6:22 Blessed are ye, when men shall hate you, and when they shall separate you from their company, and shall reproach you, and cast out your name as evil, for the Son of man's sake.]

Be happy when men hate you and men is an insult and relative to [Genesis 11:5 And the LORD came down to see the city and the tower, which the children of men builded.]

[the children of men builded.] = ones who got traditional education, written, and did not apply the fear not remedy so they were in extreme left brain state of mind, the left brain influenced containers.

So the comment"be thank"ul when men hate you and cast you out and call you evil because once you apply the remedy one uses those (bad) aspects as conditioning aspects. Right brain does not do well with praise it does well in impossible situations. This is relative to an eastern comment one does well by doing good. Doing good is what Paul was doing: [Acts 13:8 But Elymas the sorcerer (for so is his name by interpretation) withstood them, seeking to turn away the deputy from the faith.] Paul was being humiliated. Paul was going to the rulers and trying to convince them of the dangers of traditional education and some of the ruler's friends, Elymas, were mocking Paul. This pattern is similar to what Moses did. Moses did not seek a person in semi power relative to civilization he went right to the top dog the Pharaoh. It's a check mate move. If one who applies the remedy can convince a ruler of the people about the dangers of written language they win because that ruler has control over how the education is taught. This power move so to speak is a symptom of random access thinking. Moses skipped over everything and went right to the Pharaoh and Paul was skipping over everything and went right to the Governor of that location [Acts 13:7 Which was with the deputy of the country, Sergius Paulus, a prudent man; who called for Barnabas and Saul, and desired to hear the word of God.] Paul was going to the deputy of a country and Moses went right to the deputy of Egypt, the Pharaoh and perhaps just like Moses , the deputy has advisors who mocked what Moses and what Paul was saying. [Acts 13:8 But Elymas the sorcerer (for so is his name by interpretation) withstood them, seeking to turn away the deputy from the faith.] Elymas was simply a person who got the education and so Elymas did not believe the tree of knowledge was written education so he saw the tree of knowledge like many who have no applied the remedy see it, as some vague representation but not literally written language so Elymas saw the ancient texts as supernatural explanations when they are not. The ancient texts are talking about literal written language harming people's minds and then they are explaining how one can remedy that unsound state of mind. That is not supernatural that is reality cause and effect relationships. The beings in the ancient texts were saying something far more devastating than supernatural they were explaining this written language invention was turning everyone into mental nightmares and that is far beyond the realms of sinister and dark because it is everywhere. If a person who is only capable of sequential thoughts because of the education tried to imagine written language is this opiate of people's minds they would understand what a problem is, but that reality is so sinister and so devastating, their sequential thoughts cannot tie up all the loose ends, so they give up on that thought and assume it is a crazy thought. If one does not understand what this comment means relative to the tree of knowledge it is best they ponder it further. [Mark 12:38 And he said unto them in his doctrine, Beware of the scribes, which love to go in long clothing, and love salutations in the marketplaces,

[And he said unto them in his doctrine, Beware of the scribes,] This is not saying the doctrine was about supernatural he said beware of the scribes, the ones who got the education, written language, and the ones who teach it and do not suggest the remedy in conjunction with it. Granted I fell off the tracks.

Back to this movie. The main character applies the remedy, in his attempts to commit suicide after he became depressed because he understood his foot was going to be cut off. Soon he goes to an outpost of civilization, the army in this case and he meets the Indians. At first they appear strange to him but as the movie progresses he starts to see his own kind, civilization as strange. For example he has to pull all of these dead deer the previous soldiers killed and threw into a lake and he comments that he does not detect they killed the deer for food, so that is a subtle hint they killed the deer for no reason or just for fun. So slowly he starts to change is perception of who exactly is the bad one relative to the Native Americans and his own kind, civilization are. This is similar to Moses. Moses was born into civilization, Egypt, and then he came of age, applied the remedy in one way or another, and then he turned on civilization. That is a very harsh decision because anyone who turns on civilization is automatically thought to be a traitor or uncivilized because civilization denotes civility by its choice of names for itself. The deeper reality is one is under the left brain influence and then applies the re4medy and is under the right brain influence and they see how they were in that left brain influence and understand they were a beast. The point is once you apply the remedy you earn your stripes by default because you are going to be outnumbered six billion to one and that alone proves to ones who are awake to a degree you have courage no matter what anyone in civilization, left brain influenced containers, suggests contrary to that. A person who is even considering applying this remedy is a person who considering fighting Goliath. Goliath is a giant and he has vast armies behind him so a person who even considers that challenge is prone to fearlessness deep in the core of their being. It does not take any courage to fight someone you may win against, it requires courage to fight someone you understand you have no chance of defeating. The battle has never been about people who do the fighting, it is about people who fight for the children's minds so it is a selfless battle. Many of these wise beings were slaughtered trying to protect the minds of children from being bent to the left by Civilization. They did not win but they did the best they could based on the fact they were fighting against Goliath who had vast armies behind him. Why would anyone fight a battle they know they cannot win? Because a human being should protect the children's minds no matter what because the children represent the future of the species. These wise beings sacrificed their lives to protect the minds of the children from this improperly taught written language invention and now civilization celebrates that fact they killed all these wise beings with yearly feasts. The only proof one needs to understand that, is to call their local school and ask if they have an fear not conditioning to go along with all that left brain education. I have already determined to fight Goliath whether you apply the remedy or not. I have already let go so Goliath appears as nothing to me. I will attempt to work my way back into the movie now.

[Revelation 19:19 And I saw the beast, and the kings(rulers) of the earth(ones who get the education and do not apply the remedy), and their armies(minions and slaves, ones who get the education and do not apply the remedy), gathered together to make war against him that sat on the horse, and against his army(ones who got the education and did apply the remedy).]
At one point the main character is captured by his own kind, the ones who got the education and did not apply the remedy, and he is treated poorly and beaten and called a traitor. The interesting things about the title of the movie, dances with wolves, has nothing to do with the fact the main character dances with a literal wolf, it is referring to this comment in the ancient texts [Luke 10:3 Go your ways: behold, I send you forth as lambs among wolves.] Dances with wolves is the same as the David and Goliath story. The lambs are the cerebral peaceful being who are of sound mind who have applied the remedy and the wolves are the unsound minded beings who have no applied the remedy and are based on destruction. They kill these deer for fun. Later in the move it shows all the dead bison and the main character comments they killed these bison just for the tongues and that means they killed the bison just for money. The sane perceive human beings evolved from money. Things must be killed so beings can have food whether it is a plant or meat but killing things for sport or for fun is not a reason it is vanity and a waste, it is self gratification. No other animal kills other animals just for fun or sport. Only the unsound minded human beings who got the education and did not apply the remedy kill things for no reason at all. So Dances with wolves is showing a human being who got the education, left brain influenced, and accidentally applied the fear not remedy, right brain influenced, and that changed is perception from seeing civilization, left brain influenced containers, as the good guys to seeing civilization as the wolves. The main character accidentally applied the remedy and discovered he was once an ignorant beast. [Psalms 73:22 So foolish was I, and ignorant: I was as a beast before thee.] The end of the movie shows the main character moving up a mountain and away from civilization because he knew he could not convince civilization of what he discovered so he climbed the mountain, just as Moses did in the end. - 9:59:30 AM

1:21:41 PM – Constitution - Section 1 - The Legislature
All legislative Powers herein granted shall be vested in a Congress of the United States, which shall consist of a Senate and House of Representatives.
Bill of Rights - 1. Freedom of Speech, Press, Religion and Petition

Congress shall make no law respecting an establishment of religion, or prohibiting the free exercise thereof; or abridging the freedom of speech, or of the press; or the right of the people peaceably to assemble, and to petition the Government for a redress of grievances.

[Congress] = Senate and House of Representatives

Congress shall make no law abridging the freedom of speech.

The FCC deems language obscene if it incites "lustful thoughts" in the average person, describes illegal sexual acts, or as a whole lacks ...literary, artistic, political, or scientific value. The Federal Communications Commission (FCC) is an independent agency of the United States government, created, directed, and empowered by Congressional statute.

FCC = a branch of congress, empowered by congress.

Incites lustful thoughts in the average person. What they mean is, incites lustful thoughts in a person who has been conditioned to be able to maintain lustful thoughts because their mind is bent to the left as a result of many years of sequential education and a person who believes in words to begin with or is affected by words to begin with. So the FCC is empowered by congress and is allowed to determine what speech can or cannot be used so it in fact it is abridging speech but appears to be a separate entity from congress but it is not. So Congress created a branch of itself that controls speech but it appears like the FCC is not congress so it is a simple misdirection move to abridge freedom of speech.
Congress shall make no law abridging the freedom of speech. = FCC is empowered by congress so FCC shall make no law abridging freedom of speech.
[describes illegal sexual acts, or as a whole lacks ...literary, artistic, political, or scientific value.] This means this branch of congress, the FCC is able to determine what lacks literary, artistic, political and scientific value. So the FCC trumps the people's pursuit of happiness. The FCC is a judge and judges what is good and what is bad. This is simply what a tyrant does. A tyrant determines anything that does not serve its goals is bad and anything that assists it in gaining more power is good. Freedom is at the bottom of a tyrants list of good things. The FCC are people yet they are determining what is of value relative to literary, political, artistic, and scientific value and that is suggesting they assume they are all knowing. Something is presented to be played on television and the FCC determines if its contents are of value and congress empowered the FCC so congress has determined it is all knowing also.
The Bill of Rights and the Constitution created congress but now congress has assumed it created the Bill of Rights and the Constitution. The founding fathers wrote this comment the way it is because it was mindful the government, congress wants nothing more than to kill absolute freedom of speech.

Congress shall make no law abridging the freedom of speech. Some will argue there has to be censorship to keep things safe because they have yet to figure out freedom is not safe. One is never intelligent enough to be able to determine what these things are: literary, artistic, political, or scientific value. It was not of scientific value for that guy to leave a piece of bread out over night but the next day he woke up and found the mold on the bread and eventually discovered penicillin. That is the point of freedom. No one is intelligent enough to know what things that do not appear to be of literary, artistic, political, or scientific value may reveal. Many times things people have determined to be of literary, artistic, political, or scientific value are in fact not of literary, artistic, political, or scientific value. So the American people have a group of millionaire carpetbaggers determining what is of value. Congress has determined everyone is going to get the traditional education because it is of value.

I notice in homeschooling there are some states that do not require a parent to contact the state relative to the child's test scores. But then I read the fine print in one of these states that does not require a parent to keep the state abreast about the child's test scores, and the laws states.
[Children must be "instructed in subjects commonly and usually taught in the public schools" of Idaho.]
Well there is only one kind of subject usually taught in any school in America and that is hardcore sequential left brain written language and math. So this perception that home schooled children are getting something different relative to traditional education is simply an illusion.
All of the guidelines for home schooling suggest a parent can teach any topic but then they must still make sure that student passes certified accepted tests given to school attending children.
There is no mention of education in the Bill of Rights but all the sudden everyone has "o get "traditional education". The age a child must start education homeschooled or not is consistent, six or seven.
 [(All children who have attained the age of 6 years or who will have attained the age of 6 years by February 1 of any school year or who are older than 6 years of age b"t who have not attained the age of 16 years are required to attend school regularly during the entire school term.) Florida Statutes Annotated § 1003.21(1).]
[A National Institutes of Health study says the region of the brain that inhibits risky behavior is not fully formed until age 25.]
Perhaps they mean risky behavior as in a free thinker. I am mindful the education simply keeps one from thinking or inhibits thinking and at about the time one gets out of a four years college program their mind is fully inhibited of course by the age of 14 one's mind is bent all the way to the left by traditional education so anything after that is simply insult to injury. Ricky behavior would be a person who writes books explaining to the people why traditional education in fact veils right brain and leaves them as mindless specters susceptible to fear and thus simple to control with even elementary fear tactics. The rulers certainly do not

130

want to see that kind of reckless behavior but unfortunately they are no longer calling the shots anymore, so to speak.

If some aspects of the brain do not fully develop until the age of 2', 'ow can someone assume pushing all that sequential left brain education on the mind of a child is not going to affect that+" child+s ment"l development. Perhaps the most important question is why is civilization so interested in getting that child (educated) as swiftly as possible" Civiliza"ion senses time so one might suggest they are a bit impatient. One might suggest civilization wants to make that child (wise) as fast as they can. After all everyone knows traditional education is [Genesis 3:6 .. desired to make one wise] so it is best to get the children wise as fast as possible, right grasshopper? I am so humbled civilization chose to make me wise as fast as possible yet I am uncertain how I will ever repay civilization in full, but I am mindful to certainly give it my best shot. I am working on understanding the concept it is better to give than receive first hand, psychologically speaking, so to speak, and then there will be none.

[Congress shall make no law abridging the freedom of speech, or of the press] [The FCC deems language obscene if it incites "lustful thoughts" in the average person, describes illegal sexual acts, or as a whole lacks ...literary, artistic, political, or scientific value.] = making laws that inhibit freedom of press. Press = any communication venue. If one abridges freedom of speech they abridge freedom of press and if one abridges freedom of press they abridge freedom of speech. I read a comment that said freedom of speech was not created so people could run around using cuss words in public and I realized whomever wrote that fears words so they are hallucinating and delusional because they believe a sound can be bad. I bet they believe a picture can be bad. I bet they believe everything they don't like is bad.

[The FCC deems language obscene if it incites "lustful thoughts" in the average person] This comment is suggesting anything that incites thoughts in the average person. With all of the left brain education that is pushed on children there is no need to fear thoughts happening in the average person. Fear not FCC the chance of thoughts happening in the average traditionally educated person would be a miracle worthy of nothing less than a feast.

"Those who want to reap the benefits of this great nation must bear the fatigue of supporting it."
Thomas Payne

Being awake requires sacrifice but being ignorant only requires slumber. Everyone is willing to jump on the band wagon after its wheels are fixed. Supporting the nation denotes exposing the tyrants in the nation. Once a person is unable to make their own determinations they invite others to determine for them. One can do anything they determine to do except what others have determined they cannot do. One is either being manipulated or manipulating others, and one who is not aware of that is being manipulated. A great nation begins with sound minds.

"I prefer peace. But if trouble must come, let it come in my time, so that my children can live in peace. "
Thomas Payne

A tyrant that goes to war may lose his control because a citizen that goes to war against a tyrant may regain freedom in return. When control dies freedom is born. When the battle within the mind is won the tyranny in the world fades. When a tyrant loves his freedom to control a citizen fears his freedom to exist. Everyone should defeat their fear of death at least once before they are required to. Gaining respect is oft contrary to following the herd. If your enemy respects you they have become your friend. What one wants to know is in books and what one wants to understand is in life. The hardest battle is always the most rewarding battle and this keeps the rewards sparse.
Understanding is an accomplishment on its own.
Understanding yourself is not possible.
Understanding others requires understanding yourself.
Improving yourself is not a chore it is a threat.
If you listen to what others say you may start listening to what you say.
Ones value system determines ones value so always be willing to change your value system.
The mind is not concerned about what it thinks it is only concerned about thinking.
Thoughts do not have a moral code only the observers of them do. - 3:52:39 PM

Perhaps neurosis is the inability to tolerate perhaps, perhaps.

12/23/2009 2:42:47 AM – An email to someone about something.

Mark 11:18 And the scribes and chief priests heard it, and sought how they might destroy him: for they feared him, because all the people was astonished at his doctrine.

Mark 12:38 And he said unto them in his doctrine, Beware of the scribes, which love to go in long clothing, and love salutations in the marketplaces,

And the scribes... heard it, and sought how they might destroy him: = scribes = any human being who learn traditional education written language. Why did the scribes want to destroy Jesus?

Because the doctrine of the ancient texts is that written language, the tree of knowledge has unwanted mental side effects and once one gets the written language they have to apply the fear not remedy or the deny ones self remedy or the those who lose their life(mentally) preserve it..

Neurologically after one get the written language education it is all left brain sequential based so the minds bends to the left greatly and in turn the hypothalamus (the fear creator in the mind) starts sending strong signals of fear relative to.

[2 Timothy 1:7 For God hath not given us the spirit of fear; but of power, and of love, and of a sound mind.]
So this strong fear is not of God or is not natural but is caused by learning written education because the hypothalamus starts sending very strong signals of fear, embarrassment, shame, lust, greed, envy so the cure is anti fear
spirit of fear = unsound mind
fear not and loss of fear = sound mind = [For God hath not given us the spirit of fear; but of sound mind.]

So Abraham was the first to suggest fear not as a remedy to this spirit of fear caused by the mind being bent to the left
by learning written language
[Genesis 15:1 After these things the word of the LORD came unto Abram in a vision, saying, Fear not, Abram: I am thy shield, and thy exceeding great reward.]
Fear not the one gets an exceeding great reward. What is that reward? They unveil their right brain, the right hand side, and return to sound mind and lose that spirit of fear.

So this is why this comment was made [Mark 12:38 And he said unto them in his doctrine, Beware of the scribes] Beware of the ones who get the education , written language and have not applied the remedy, the scribes. END

12/23/2009 6:28:02 PM – Once upon a time a human being accidentally awoke from the mental neurosis caused by learning the written language, the tree of knowledge. He attempted to explain the truth he had discovered to others about the written language. Over many years other beings started to wake up and they attempted to explain how the initial being was proper in his explanations. Eventually one being woke up and he could explain it to the multitudes and no one found fault with his explanations and he had a group of disciples who were also very adept at explaining the dangers of the written language if not taught properly. The scribers and rulers soon caught wind of this being and his disciples and they plotted against him. Eventually the scribes found a way to snare him and his group of disciples and the scribes were set on making an example of him. So every year in the dead of winter, to represent the cold hearts of the scribes, the scribes have feasts and materialistic celebrations to warn any being who wakes up from the neurosis to keep their mouth shut or they will suffer the same fate as the ones who woke up before them. And in the spring the scribes celebrate killing these wise beings because everything the scribes do is backwards and so the scribes celebrate death in the spring and life in the winter. The scribes made sure all the children joined in their feasts. Other beings woke up and also tried to fight against the scribes valiantly but the scribe's numbers were great. In time one being woke up from the neurosis caused by the script and that being had all the proper words to use to explain to the world the methods of the scribes and many of the ruler scribes hearts grew heavy because they realized they never did kill the truth and their feasts celebrating their defeat of the truth did not frighten the truth but only made the truth more determined.

10:16:54 PM – An email to someone about something.

[Mark 3:29 But he that shall blaspheme against the Holy Ghost hath never forgiveness, but is in danger of eternal damnation:]

Neurologically speaking written language, the tree of knowledge is sequential based. The first thing a child does in education is memorize the ABC's. This is a sequential favoring process. Eventually a child is taught to spell and that is nothing but arranging letters in sequential order and the children that spell well are rewarded and the children that do not spell well are punished with bad grades. So this is simply carrot and stick conditioning. The better a child does at the sequential left brain aspects the more praise they are given by the scribes, the teachers of the script.

So this comment [Genesis 1:27 So God created man in his own image,...]
is explaining the right brain aspect of the spirit is the God image and the traditional education in favoring left brain in turn veils right brain, the god image so to speak so in turn one who veils this right brain god image in children under the guise of traditional education sins against the holy spirit.

[[Mark 3:29 But he that shall blaspheme against the Holy Ghost hath never forgiveness, but is in danger of eternal damnation:]

But the clarification is the ones who do this to children also had it done to them, so as Jesus explained, They know not what they do. This means it is rare for a person to ever be aware this "conditioning" happen to them because it is very subtle and after perhaps five or six years of the traditional education their mind/spirit starts bending to the left so they cannot even tell this has happened to them because it started when they were six and so their mind was never fully developed so they could tell it was happening to them.

So once in a while one of these beings has an accident and "wakes up" from that education conditioning and tries to explain it to the ones who have not yet woken up but because that being has to explain it is caused by written education, the tree

134

of knowledge it is not readily accepted because written education is thought to be without flaws and if a person tries to understand it is simply a tool with some major flaws relative to what it can do to the spirit/mind of a child if not taught properly, they would perhaps have to reevaluate everything and so many do not want to face that truth. - 10:17:19 PM

10:41:50 PM - Even early on after the accident I always felt I was going with the flow. I felt I was a rabbit that was hit by a truck and I had no choice but to go with the mac truck that hit me. This is an indication how powerful right brain is because it actually makes a person who has had it veiled their whole life feel as if right brain is not even them. It makes one feel after they unveil right brain as if right brain is something else totally separate. This is relative to contrast, one is adjust from having a mental tricycle to having a shuttle booster rocket mentally and so that contrast is so great the being has to adjust for a long time to that. But the word adjust sounds like its work or it takes effort but in reality one just goes with the flow and lets the current carry them. This is what I suggested early on is the progression stage. I recall I would say "I have progressed" about every five minutes relative to a clock early on after the accident because right brain learns so fast with its pattern detection and intuition and speed of thought processing that one is mentally a sponge for nearly the first six to eight months after they unveil right brain. One is not able to do anything mentally but learn and the more they learn the more right brain seeks more things to learn. It is not seeking to learn because it wants to finish it is seeking to learn to warm itself up. Right brain is not even concerned with getting things wrong because it sometimes gets things wrong so it can ponder that situation more carefully and then adjust and finds its mistake and that also is learning or finding new understandings. That is perhaps the best way to look at right brain, it's a machine that only wants to find another understanding and that means a mistake can become an understanding and getting something correct can be an understanding so a mistake and getting something correct are the same thing to right brain. I am aware of many loose ends that I do not cover because right brain always leaves loose ends for future exploration and so right brain is not looking to come to a conclusion as much as it is looking to create more branches to explore. I knew none of these things I write about before that accident so that proves I am not an authority and I am learning just as much as anyone from the writing so I am being taught. Right brain is just a flood gate and once it opens the being is unable to swim against that flood of learning and processing and understanding so they appear to be speaking of right brain as a separate entity but perhaps that is only because they are not use to such powerful processing. There is very little electrical current going through the brain but the amount of cerebral output the right brain creates makes it seem like there is some kind of energy to output ratio that defies physics going on. It is like a million mainframe computers running on a 9 volt battery and it so efficient one never even senses any fatigue or hunger or stress. I am not bragging about me I am bragging about right brain and so I am in fact bragging about us, every single human being has this right brain it just has to be unveiled. The point is not to unveil right brain or that is not the end of the story the real story happens after one unveils right brain and then tries to explain how powerful it is. So far I can suggest its power in unnamable. After 13 books I am still sitting on, right brain power is unnamable. So that means I really have not accomplished anything but I am diligent in not accomplishing anything. The one aspect of right brain is that the heavier the burden is perceives the better it gets and so it is always trying to sense an infinite burden because that's means it will become infinity better and that is an endless cycle. This shows a lot of validity to the concept written language is nothing more than a way to dumb us down for whatever reason. What would our species do if we all unveiled right brain and solved all our problems swiftly? Perhaps the greatest fear is that we would ponder ourselves into silence. I do not communicate with many beings who have applied the remedy and unveiled right brain because we simply do not have much to talk about. All there is to talk about is the ones who have not applied the remedy and methods to get them to apply the remedy to unveil their right brain. So I am reduced to talking to myself and when I want to get my teeth kicked in I talk to the ones who have not applied the remedy. This is relative to Moses in a sense at the end Moses went off to be alone way up on the mountain, the wise man on top of the mountain all alone by himself. So Moses finally pondered himself into silence. Right brain did everything it could to reach the people he tried to teach and then finally it just no longer talks out loud and so everything is reduced to cerebral thoughts. There are no more words left to say and the mind just goes into cerebral thoughts which are not even fully explainable in words. The right brain complexity and calculations and paradox are so fast that words simply cannot explain that level of cerebral processing. There are not enough words to explain the complexity so one goes into silence and stops using words all together. So when one unveils right brain they are a motor mouth but that is because they are in fact pondering their way into silence and so they must fight to avoid pondering their self into silence because they are mindful they must try to wake their friends and they can only do that with words. Their friends are in the world of words and they are in the world of cerebral communication so they must fight to remain in the world of verbal communicate for the sake of their friends. This struggle creates a nice epic battle. Even the ones who apply the remedy must seek self control to avoid the traps in the neutral mindset, they are on another level but they are never at the top because there is no top, only flat ground. One being who has not applied the remedy said to me "If everyone applied the remedy we would all just sit around and do nothing." That is in fact great truth because we would revert back to communicating cerebrally and since cerebral communication is not tangible we would be doing nothing. We would return to being and leave becoming; cerebral beings that look at physical aspects as necessity instead of physical based beings looking at cerebral aspects as difficulty. This is all relative to the lack of purpose aspect. Our species makes things so hard on itself to give it the illusion of purpose because we are aware on some deep seeded level we have no purpose. Having no purpose means we can relax a little bit but having this illusion of purpose makes us do things in a rush and that only makes things harder on us.

[Genesis 1:25 And God made the beast of the earth after his kind, and cattle after their kind, and every thing that creepeth upon the earth after his kind: and God saw that it was good.]

We are trying to make things good when they are already good, so we only make things bad. We want to have purpose so badly it is harming us because no purpose is a void and we try so hard to fill that void that can never be filled so the only solution is to relax and go with the flow and stop trying to fight the void because one will only tire their self out and never get anywhere fighting a void.

[Genesis 1:2 And the earth was without form, and void;]

The answers are seldom what one wants them to be but they are still the answers. In a void one creates their own purpose and their own pursuit of happiness and thus their own meaning.

Our brains are so powerful we reached a point of understanding that we became aware of reality itself and the only solution to escape that awareness was to become ignorant because we could not change the fact our brains were so powerful, so we had to find a way to make them less powerful and so we altered our perception and went back down a level because the mental level were at naturally was a level we did not wish to be at. The level we went down to by altering our perception gave us a chance to find out what reality is again. As a species we will eventuality discover reality again and then we will seek to alter our perception in order to go down a level from there and start the process over again. A being that is aware of reality seeks to escape that awareness. Our minds are so intelligent we cannot escape them we can only hinder them to give us the illusion of accomplishment. We are all trying to find out who is most intelligent because we cannot handle the fact we are most intelligent. It is lonely at the top so we seek to throw ourselves back in the mix to make it a race again. We always win the race because we are the only ones in the race. We try to find something greater than ourselves because we are afraid we will be all alone if we do not. Intelligence is achieved when one understands everyone is equally intelligent but just has different ways of showing it. There are infinite ways of showing our intelligence and so we are infinitely intelligent. Ignorance is not a symptom of stupidity but a symptom a vastly intelligent being is seeking purpose. Until we understand we are far too intelligent we will continue to harm ourselves in our attempts to become more intelligent. We get tangled up in our vast intelligence because we never quite understood what it meant when they suggest our brains are very large for our size. Our brains are far larger than a dinosaurs but we do not grasp that means we are way to intelligent for our own good. We are blessed with too much intelligence and that is our curse. We try to make a child intelligent but one cannot make a child intelligent because they are far too intelligent to begin with, so one only harms them. We cannot understand the concept leave well enough alone. Our species has already solved the mystery but we are just going through a rerun to have something to do. We are watching the movie again because that is all we have left to do. A bird in the sky see's a human and is pleased he is not as intelligent as we are. The only way we can understand we are too intelligent is to become aware we are harming ourselves and we are not even aware of it because we think we are helping ourselves. We

invent the internet and it collapses entire industries so we harm our self as much as we help our self. The only solution is to relax and be mindful the more we do the more tangled we become. Our progress denotes we are progressing to become more tangled in our own complexity. We all understand the environment is not what it used to be 1000 years ago because of us, but we are not aware that our own desire to progress is in reality our undoing. We are only progressing further into the tangle. We are not progressing out of the tangle. We have altered our perception and so we are unable to see exactly what we are doing. We need the intuition of right brain to be able to sense what is happening and sense what the results of our actions are. There is no book that is going to explain the results of our actions so we need the intuition to judge our own actions and that means we are on a tight rope. We have to be honest observers of our own deeds as a species so that our deeds do not fall back on us. There are no other creatures we can ask to be honest observers of us but us and so we are a biased judge of our own deeds. We can learn from our mistakes but first we must remember our mistakes. We must judge ourselves and that means we are prone to corrupted judgment. We altered our perceptions as the result of an invention, which was a symptom of our vast intelligence 5000 years ago, and as a species we are not even mindful of that yet. We are 5000 years into a trap we set for ourselves, and we are still not at the level of being mindful we did something to ourselves as a result of our vast intelligence, unknowingly. It was an honest mistake but we are biased observers of our own deeds so we are unwilling to judge ourselves in an unbiased manner. We have to judge our deeds and inventions in an unbiased fashion because no one else has the intelligence to judge our deeds. Our very nature is to fight each other because nothing else is a challenge but our selves. We are the heavyweight champion with no one to fight so we are imploding from boredom. We are harming each other and ourselves because we annihilated all the other species. That is logical since we are the champion. The frustration is not from having too much challenge it is from having no challenge. We are looking for a mountain on flat ground and we will do anything to find it. It is the flat ground that frightens us, not the mountain.
- 12/24/2009 1:06:50 AM

[Luke 20:46 Beware of the scribes, which desire to walk in long robes, and love greetings in the markets, and the highest seats in the synagogues, and the chief rooms at feasts;]

12/24/2009 9:03:26 PM — [Luke 1:2 Even as they delivered them unto us, which from the beginning were eyewitnesses, and ministers of the word;]

Eyewitnesses denotes beings who got the written education and then in one way or another broke free of it or applied the remedy. This suggests the contrast. Only one who applies the remedy can attest to the contrast of how they were and how they are after the remedy. Some say, I once was lost but now am found. Some say I was blind but now I see. Some say I was dead but now I am resurrected. These are witnesses because they understand the contrast. A person who does not apply the remedy has no idea what the contrast is. Many who get the traditional education assume their mind is just fine because they are clueless understandably because their mind was bent to the left when they were a child so they could not possible know the difference from a mind bent to the left to a mind that applies the remedy and unveils right brain.

[Psalms 73:22 So foolish was I, and ignorant: I was as a beast before thee.] = a witness

[Jeremiah 50:6 My people hath been lost sheep: their shepherds have caused them to go astray, they have turned them away on the mountains: they have gone from mountain to hill, they have forgotten their restingplace.]

[My people hath been lost sheep] = people who got the written education and did not apply the remedy

[their shepherds have caused them to go astray] = the rulers of civilization, ruler left brain influenced container, the ones who gave them the written education improperly and veiled their right brain knowingly or unknowingly.

[they have turned them away on the mountains: they have gone from mountain to hill] = Because their right brain was veiled they went from cerebral giants to cerebral jokes. Mountain in this comment denotes great heights , great wisdom, great understanding, and then their right brain was veiled and then they were simple minded and just men instead of Masters of the house/ mind.

[they have forgotten their restingplace.] = This denotes their minds were bent to the left as children and they have forgotten how they were as children when right brain was unveiled. They walk around assuming they are not the greatest mind in the universe because their mind was taken from them when they were so young they simply do not even remember. They believe because they failed a few sequential tests it means they are stupid and so they are lost. They have no way to get back to how they were because they do not even understand they are lost so these witnesses are the ones who try to remind them how to get back to their restingplace. The cerebral powerhouse place, where the mental suffering stops. The witnesses try to gently coax them out of hell where they have fallen and get them back to grace where they were before they had fallen. It's like herding cats into the water.

[Luke 19:10 For the Son of man is come to seek and to save that which was lost.] What is a son of man? A person any person who got the education given by men and then applied the remedy and then becomes a witness and tries to wake up the lost who have not applied the remedy.

Man is relative to this comment [Genesis 11:5 And the LORD came down to see the city and the tower, which the children of men builded.]

So a child of man or a son of man is a person who gets the written education.

[children of men] = son of man

[the Son of man is come to seek] The word seek is relative to the wheat in contrast to the chaff. A seeker hears the comments and they want to know more and so their cup is empty and they wish to fill it. The chaff have a full cup and so they only wish to doubt or argue so they are not seekers. A scientist for example is a seeker because they run experiments not because they know the end result but because they seek understanding. The ones with a full cup tend to be the ones closer to the first circle of hell relative to Dante's inferno and the seekers tend to be much closer to the 9th circle of hell which means they are the meek and the poor in spirit. So this comment [the Son of man is come to seek] is suggesting a son of man, one who gets the written education, seeks and then they apply the remedy and then they [save that which was lost.], their right brain and become a witness and then they tell others so that other seekers can [save that which was lost.] which means apply the remedy, also. It is a sort of endless loop. A son of man gets the education then the ones who are seekers will hear about the remedy and understand why it is important and apply the remedy and then they will tell others and convince them to apply the remedy.

[Matthew 3:11 I indeed baptize you with water unto repentance: but he that cometh after me is mightier than I, whose shoes I am not worthy to bear: he shall baptize you with the Holy Ghost, and with fire:] This is John the Baptist talking and he has applied the remedy so he is being very meek and humble and the reason he can be like this is because he has no ego and the words do not work on one who has applied the remedy. The deeper reality is John understood Herod was coming for him so he was grooming his successor.

This is when Jesus applied the remedy. [Matthew 3:16 And Jesus, when he was baptized, went up straightway out of the water: and, lo, the heavens were opened unto him, and he saw the Spirit of God descending like a dove, and lighting upon him:] and this is when John was taken away to be killed by the cult, civilization [Matthew 4:12 Now when Jesus had heard that John was cast into prison, he departed into Galilee;] and so Jesus left the area because he knew they would get him also.

One of the first stages after you apply the remedy is this sensation which could be called paranoid or fear that you may go back to how you were. I said Thank you way too much and I said perhaps way to much relative to this paranoia I would lose this great right brain aspect I just unveiled. Some people do not even use written language after they apply the remedy and this is the paranoia that it may make them go back to how they were or condition them again. This is an indication how powerful right brain is once it is unveiled, it is like finding the greatest thing in the universe and then one is paranoid they may lose it so they do anything they are compelled to do relative to making sure they do not lose it. Early on I was known in some chat rooms as the guy who never says anything because all of my sentences were like this. Perhaps I say perhaps too much perhaps. This is not a permanent thing this is an early stage after one applies the remedy and unveils right brain. It is a scale on both ends. One has to go through the mental hell circles to get to the 9th circle of hell, treason then they are in the mindset and apply remedy then they unveiled right brain and then there are circles of "heaven" one has to go through so this paranoia of losing right brain after it is unveiled is just an early circle or stage on the heaven, consciousness aspect side. These stages pass very swiftly as long as one applies the remedy to full measure, defeats their fear of death but if one goes the slow route, perhaps uses other methods like simply meditating not in a cemetery for example or just says perhaps a lot they

may be stuck at one of these stages for a long period of time. That is the reason for going the full measure. "Those who lose their life will preserve it" , "Tho I walk through the valley of the shadow of death I fear no evil." Those are the full measure remedies. Fear not is a full measure remedy because some who apply the remedy but not fully can get stuck in one of the circles on the "heaven" side. There is a circle of supernatural perception one goes through and this is because one is unable to explain to their self how powerful right brain is so they assume it must be supernatural but then as long as one progresses they will eventually understand all the traits they are exhibiting are traits of right brain. Ambiguity, intuition, paradox, complexity are all right brain traits and so as long as they keep progressing they come out of the supernatural stage and achieve the stage "Oh it's all just right brain traits and right brain is unnamable in power." There are people in history who get stuck in the supernatural stage and they end up with a God complex. One can look at it like a child who says "I am superman." Children have scenarios and games where they are the most powerful thing in the universe and they have games where they always end up winning in the end. That's a right brain trait. Right brain does not have an ego or pride so it has no limits so once it is unveiled one will come across as having an infinite ego because they have no way of telling what is too much ego and they also start to lose their belief or fear of words. One of the first stages is adjust to no sense of time. One will rush around and make tons of mistakes because with no sense of time they cannot even tell they are rushing around but that is just stage and they will warm up so to speak and right brain is a master at adaptation so they adapt to all of these situations and sort them out. It is not about being perfect in the eyes of others it a personal experience. One is bettering their self by making these mistakes and then looking at them and adjusting and mistakes do not mean anything to one with no ego because right brain see's mistakes as a chance to come to understandings. Ones conditioned into extreme left brain are afraid to ever make a mistake or give the impression they make dumb mistakes, and right brain makes its living off of experimenting and in an experiment there can never be a mistake. The complexity is one has only unveiled right brain back to 50% power in harmony with left brain and that means one exhibits symptoms of both left and right brain. Think about how you are now and then add in complexity, random access thoughts, strong intuition, paradox and loads of creativity to your thoughts and that's how your mind will be after the remedy. So this remedy is not favoring right brain it is simply unlocking it after it was veiled from all those years of sequential left brain education. So one is going from an unsound state of mind back to a sound state of mind they had as a child. One has to go through this remedy in order to get back to where they once belonged or get back to [their restingplace.] which is sanity. This is serious yet also humor.
[1 Samuel 9:20 And as for thine asses that were lost three days ago, set not thy mind on them; for they are found. And on whom is all the desire of Israel? Is it not on thee, and on all thy father's house?]
This comment is saying this [Psalms 73:22 So foolish was I, and ignorant: I was as a beast before thee.]

[And as for thine asses that were lost three days ago, set not thy mind on them; for they are found.] = [So foolish was I, and ignorant: I was as a beast before thee.] = I once was lost and now am found. = I once was blind but now I see.

This comment [And as for thine asses that were lost three days ago, set not thy mind on them; for they are found.] is also relative to the comment past is past. After one applies the remedy they will not be able to recall or relate to how they were before in the extreme left brain state. You did not do anything in your life before you applied the remedy that was out of bounds relative to a person who was conditioned as a child into an unsound, insane mental state. You were a child and civilization, the cult, put you in that unsound mental state and so whatever you did, no longer matters so do not set your mind on those deeds because after you apply the remedy you are found, and that is all that important. You did the best you could based on the fact civilization raped you into mental hell so don't sweat it, just be pleased you applied the remedy. You will need all the concentration you can muster in your efforts to convince civilization it should stop mentally raping children by teaching them traditional education improperly. The deeper reality is you will not be able to mentally relate to how you were before you unveil right brain. The memories will be there but the emotions and time stamps will be gone so it will be like looking at a picture, but a very distanced picture, like a past life. The deepest reality is the "rulers" in civilization know not what they do to the children and that means they are insane because civilization did to them the same thing it did to you. Lunatic things happen in a lunatic asylum. Of course I am in infinite denial traditional education is nothing more than a tool to make a person mentally dull and susceptible to fear tactics and thus easy to control. That is perhaps fact but you are not going to do anything about it but take the pain of knowing that. The cult, left brain influenced containers, has all the weapons, the law on their side and billions of minions who will kill you and then brag about how wise they are for doing so. The cult brags about how many children it educates so you know it brags about killing children, so your death will not even be brag worthy to the cult.

CD. (15) allegedly shot herself because she was about to be sent to rehab. This child became addicted to drugs just to get some relief from being conditioned into an unsound state of mind and then when she saw the prospects of how her life was going she opted to just check out and civilization, the cult, will Babylon into infinity about how its "brand" of education had nothing to with this, because the cult is pure darkness. Adam said better than I will ever able to say it.
[Genesis 2:17 But of the tree of the knowledge of good and evil, thou shalt not eat of it: for in the day that thou eatest thereof thou shalt surely die.]

I was trying to play my video game but now I have something more to say.
[tree of the knowledge of good and evil] = written education, sequential based, bents the mind to the left, sequential based, and one starts seeing parts, good and evil for example so then ones perception is unsound because a mind divided cannot stand or a hallucinating mind is an unsound mind.
'A house divided against itself cannot stand." - Abraham Lincoln

[divided against itself] the mind, in the extreme left brain state see's parts, so it sees things it should be neutral towards as either good or evil.

So C.D. did drugs to get relief from that extreme left brain state. She perceived the drugs were good so she keep doing them. Her peers saw the drugs as bad so they told C.D. she was evil for doing the drugs. So C.D. saw her peers as evil because she saw the drugs as good. So then C.D. became addicted the drugs and saw that as evil and then she saw rehab as evil and before she knew it everything around her was evil and she determined it was because she was evil and so she decided to check out. C.D. perceived she was evil because everyone around her told her drugs are evil and since she liked the drugs and they gave her relief from the extreme left brain state she concluded she was evil and it was best to kill herself. So in this extreme left brain state one is either going to end up harming their self seeking things they perceive are good or trying to stop things they perceive are evil. Now if a person see's a child being raped and they see that as evil that is righteous and that is not a hallucination. A drug is inanimate so that cannot be evil. A rock is not evil or good unless it is sitting in the center of Goliaths forehead then it is an exceptionally lucky rock. A person may see that going 90 miles an hour in a car while drunk is fun or good when it is really dangerous but that person will still do it under the guise of it is fun. The fun sensation is really a right brain sensation one gets when they break rules. Left brain is rule based right brain is anti rules so when one breaks rules they feel a sensation mentally. This sensation is what one should always have when their right brain is unveiled but since their right brain was veiled by traditional education being taught improperly that person has to do dangerous things to get that sensation and sometimes it costs them their life. Thrill seekers are simply human beings that had their right brain veiled and they do things to feel right brain for a moment and sometimes they die as a result. So to want to feel right brain after it has been veiled is good, one should not have had it veiled to begin with so that person is seeking to feel right brain but going about it in a fashion that may kill them. This is exactly what drug addiction is. A drug user likes to feel right brain and that is all the drugs do is unveil right brain while the drugs last and that is righteous to want to feel right brain but they are going about it in a fashion that sometimes kills them. So the reverse thing here is, civilization is punishing drug users for seeking to feel right brain after civilization has veiled that person's right brain with its "brand" of education. One cannot say it any better than this.

[Ephesians 5:18 And be not drunk with wine, wherein is excess; but be filled with the Spirit;]

You like thrill seeking and like the sensation of being high? Apply the remedy and you always be high and always have the sensation of this adrenalin rush and you will not risk killing yourself literally as a result of seeking to feel those sensations. It will take at least eight months just to get use to how high you are if you apply the remedy to the full measure. I assure you no matter what drugs you have been on they only let you feel right brain just a little bit and just for the duration the drug lasts. When you feel right brain unveil "Hit by a truck" is about the only thing you will saying for about the next eight months. Doing drugs is a

143

method of unveiling right brain and that is a fact but one can do it much easier and in one second if they simply get into a situation that makes that hypothalamus send them the perceived death signal and then a person closes their eyes and says to their self "I don't care I am not running I ignore that signal." That takes one second and it on a thought level and one in the extreme left brain state is afraid of everything so it's very easy to find the right situation to get that hypothalamus to send that death signal. What this drug addiction the world has and that includes caffeine and many other drugs used to pep one up or pep one down is a symptom the world has their mind bent to the left. Coffee does not work once right brain is unveiled. When ones wake up in the morning they are wide awake so they have no reason to drink coffee and even if they drank 10 cups in one minute they would feel no more awake. So coffee consumption is a symptom one has been mentally bent to the left. So one has to actually do drugs to feel what sanity is like and that is how insane they are in that left brain extreme state. So people who do drugs are subconsciously, right brain, trying to wake their self up and most end up killing their self trying to wake up but the deeper reality is when right brain is veiled it is going to get itself unveiled even if it kills the person in the process.

This is the proof - CD. (15) allegedly shot herself because she was about to be sent to rehab. It is simply cause and effect. Right brain will sometimes kill a person trying to get out and if it does not it may be that person's right brain was so veiled it is essentially dead. Even an obese person who overeats is a symptom right brain is trying to get out because to that person when they eat certain foods or a lot of foods, that lets them feel right brain, it's a cerebral sensation and they like that sensation so they eat and eat and eat until they die.

Jesus did not say drugs are bad. [Ephesians 5:18 And be not drunk with wine, wherein is excess; but be filled with the Spirit;] He said drugs are in excess which means they work at unveiling right brain but it does not have to be that difficult. Buddha did not come back and say go starve for 39 or 43 days because he was mindful it does not have to be that difficult. Just go make that hypothalamus send you that perceived death signal and then ignore it. I am not suggesting you have to take a handful of anti depressants to get that death signal because I am mindful it does not need to be that difficult. Many are afraid of scary movies and that is perhaps enough to get that hypothalamus to send that death signal if they for example go into the bathroom and turn out the lights all alone and look in the mirror. This fear not remedy is all mental and not physical. Don't jump into a shark frenzy because that is in excess. This fear not remedy is mental suicide but that is only relative to one who perceives being in extreme left brain unsound state of mind is life. In reality the remedy is how one reaches mental life and that denotes the extreme left brain state is mental death. Those who lose their life will preserve it, which means those who lose the death state of mind enter the life state of mind. Now I will go ponder my next infinite vanity lesson while playing the video game. - 12/25/2009 12:09:29 AM

2:58:59 AM – It is very important you understand I am not suggesting you have to apply this remedy. I am not suggesting you will go to "hell" after you die if you do not apply this remedy. In fact the extreme left brain state one is in after all that traditional education is hell, the place of suffering, so all one can do is attempt to get out of hell if they decide to. Hell is the absence of God and that means the education veils right brain so right brain it is absent from ones thoughts, reduced to a subconscious state.

9:41:17 AM – There are the children who are suicidal at around the age of 14 to 18 and they are the ones who did not take well to the education. These children are in the 9th circle of hell, treason, yet they have only been alive for a very short period. They are not even 20 and they are already in the 9th circle of hell mentally. They are already openly trying to kill their self and they are not even adults yet and this is because all that sequential education has done something terrible to them. Some hang on for years and years in that 9th circle until they eventually end up going through with the suicide and some cannot hang on very long before going through with the suicide. These beings are infinitely meek by the age of 20 and the cult looks at them as being bad seeds. Their parents have no clue why they are the way they are and the psychologist only answer is to throw drugs at the child as long as they get plenty of kickbacks from the pharmaceutical companies for doing so. These young meek beings start to become aware everyone around them is insane and perhaps they are the only sane one they know. They are less than 20 years old and they are already ready to die and I am mindful I perhaps cannot help them because once one is in the 9th circle which is treason at such a young age they feel they have already seen everything in this place and all they wish to do is hedge their bets that death will offer something a bit more comforting. I apologize to the young beings for the scribes, civilization, the ones under the left brain influence, because I am mindful the scribes will not be apologizing to you. I assure you little ones the scribes know not what they do. I perhaps am not intelligent enough to sway the scribes, little ones, or perhaps I am, perhaps. - 9:53:20 AM

[Matthew 7:29 For he taught them as one having authority, and not as the scribes.]
[Matthew 9:3 And, behold, certain of the scribes said within themselves, This man blasphemeth.]

[Revelation 5:5 And one of the elders saith unto me, Weep not: behold, the Lion of the tribe of Juda, the Root of David, hath prevailed to open the book, and to loose the seven seals thereof.]

"In the darkest hole, you'd be well advised
Not to plan my funeral before the body dies, yeah."
Alice in Chains – Grind

It is done. Tis Well

12/25/2009 00:00:00 AM